Ann Arbor District Library

3 1621 2102 1 1336

WITHDRAWN

D1482692

Additional Praise for
*The Little Book of Big Profits
from Small Stocks*

"Hilary Kramer is one of the best-known investors in America. In this book, her personal recipe for making money on Wall Street is finally revealed."

—Matthew Valencia, U.S. Finance Editor, *The Economist*

"Hilary Kramer is bold and daring—giving readers the courage to try a new approach to achieve the life-changing investment returns that all investors truly crave."

—Paul Taylor, Business Technology Editor, *Financial Times*

"In this fast-moving, valuable and perceptive book, Hilary Kramer shows readers how to find great undiscovered growth stocks. She has just the right message for turbulent times."

—James K. Glassman, financial columnist, *Kiplinger's Personal Finance,* and former Undersecretary of State

"Hilary Kramer's *Little Book* is bound to have a big impact on your finances. It's full of smart advice and real-life stock-picking stories about companies you know—Ford, Priceline, and Cabela's among them."

—Tyler Mathisen, noted business TV anchor

"Fun to read and easy to understand, Hilary Kramer's *Little Book* is filled with smart advice that is empowering and immediately actionable. This is a game-changer for anyone interested in being a richly successful personal investor."

—Joe Peyronnin, Cofounder of Fox News Channel and NYU Professor of Journalism

"For years, Hilary Kramer has been pulling back the curtain to reveal how to make money in the stock market, and she does it again in this book."

—Andrea Coombes, Personal Finance Editor, *MarketWatch*, and Wall Street Journal Digital Network

"Kramer's rock-solid picking acumen has both earned her clients' countless amounts of money, and protected them, too. Kramer's investing advice is as vital as oxygen."

—Elizabeth MacDonald, Fox Business

"This is one of the liveliest, fun to read, and informative books on investing that I have ever read."

—Wallace Forbes, CFA, president of the Forbes Investors Advisory Institute

"Big ideas don't come cheap. But big ideas start off small and Hilary has a sharp eye finding them when they're bargains."

—Tom Hudson, *Nightly Business Report* on PBS

"Over the years, during good markets and bad, Hilary has demonstrated an uncanny ability to research and recommend investment strategies that work. This book is mandatory reading for anyone who has watched their money wither rather than flourish."

—Ken and Daria Dolan, former cohosts of one of America's most-listened-to nationally syndicated personal finance radio show

THE LITTLE BOOK

OF
BIG PROFITS FROM
SMALL STOCKS

Little Book Big Profits Series

In the *Little Book Big Profits* series, the brightest icons in the financial world write on topics that range from tried-and-true investment strategies to tomorrow's new trends. Each book offers a unique perspective on investing, allowing the reader to pick and choose from the very best in investment advice today.

Books in the *Little Book Big Profits* series include:

THE LITTLE BOOK

OF

BIG PROFITS FROM
SMALL STOCKS

Why You'll Never Buy a Stock

Over $10 Again

HILARY KRAMER

WILEY

John Wiley & Sons, Inc.

Copyright © 2012 by InvestorPlace Media, LLC. All rights reserved.

Published by John Wiley & Sons, Inc., Hoboken, New Jersey.
Published simultaneously in Canada.

No part of this publication may be reproduced, stored in a retrieval system, or transmitted in any form
or by any means, electronic, mechanical, photocopying, recording, scanning, or otherwise, except as
permitted under Section 107 or 108 of the 1976 United States Copyright Act, without either the prior
written permission of the Publisher, or authorization through payment of the appropriate per-copy fee
to the Copyright Clearance Center, Inc., 222 Rosewood Drive, Danvers, MA 01923, (978) 750-8400,
fax (978) 646-8600, or on the Web at www.copyright.com. Requests to the Publisher for permission
should be addressed to the Permissions Department, John Wiley & Sons, Inc., 111 River Street,
Hoboken, NJ 07030, (201) 748-6011, fax (201) 748-6008, or online at www.wiley.com/go/permissions.

Limit of Liability/Disclaimer of Warranty: While the publisher and author have used their best efforts
in preparing this book, they make no representations or warranties with respect to the accuracy or com-
pleteness of the contents of this book and specifically disclaim any implied warranties of merchantability
or fitness for a particular purpose. No warranty may be created or extended by sales representatives or
written sales materials. The advice and strategies contained herein may not be suitable for your situation. You should consult with a professional where appropriate. Neither the publisher nor author shall
be liable for any loss of profit or any other commercial damages, including but not limited to special,
incidental, consequential, or other damages.

For general information on our other products and services or for technical support, please contact our
Customer Care Department within the United States at (800) 762-2974, outside the United States at
(317) 572-3993 or fax (317) 572-4002.

Wiley also publishes its books in a variety of electronic formats. Some content that appears in print
may not be available in electronic books. For more information about Wiley products, visit our web site
at www.wiley.com.

Library of Congress Cataloging-in-Publication Data:

Kramer, Hilary.
   The little book of big profits from small stocks : why you'll never buy a stock over $10 again /
Hilary Kramer.
      p. cm. — (Little book big profits series)
      ISBN 978-1-118-15005-4 (hardback); 978-1-118-19803-2 (ebk)l 978-1-118-19802-5 (ebk);
   978-1-118-19761-5 (ebk)
      1. Small capitalization stocks.   2. Investments.   I. Title.
   HG4971.K73   2011
   332.63'22—dc23   2011034200

Printed in the United States of America
10 9 8 7 6 5 4 3 2 1

Contents

Foreword

I FIND IT REFRESHING THAT INVESTING VETERAN HILARY Kramer has taken the time to share her over 25 years of Wall Street experience with Main Street individual investors like you. Her tours of duty include stints at Morgan Stanley and Lehman Brothers during their heydays, as well as starting up and managing a multimillion-dollar hedge fund.

Hilary is certainly no stranger to Wall Street and will be the first to tell you that she attributes much of her career success to investing in low-priced beaten-down stocks. And in reading this book, it's clear her goal is to help you achieve similar success.

If you come prepared, the stock market is a great place to build your wealth. Hilary puts extra emphasis on the *if you come prepared* part. These days, looking up investing tips and information on the web is as easy as powering up your PC and running a quick search. The trouble with doing so is that most of what you'll find won't actually help you succeed. In fact, much of what you'll find can often do more harm than good, especially when it comes to advice about investing in small, low-priced stocks.

One of the first lessons you'll learn in this little book is the significance of Wall Street's herd instinct. When something excites or scares Wall Street, a stampede into or out of shares can overpower a stock. I've seen it first-hand, and can tell you that investing on the right side of that stampede can lead to incredible profits.

Hilary will show you how Wall Street's herd instinct is especially powerful in moving low-priced stocks. There's no denying the impressive gains of the real-world stock stories she dispenses chapter after chapter. You can't help but look at the stock chart of a company like Darling International with anything but admiration.

Of course, as anyone who has worked on Wall Street will tell you, investing in low-priced stocks takes know-how. What I like is that Hilary's approach is honest and direct in not only making the case for these types of stocks, but also warning readers of the potential dangers to avoid.

It's evident that her approach is one of knowledge is power, as she goes to great lengths to arm readers with step-by-step instructions on how to hunt for those low-priced stocks that are poised to breakout. I think readers of this little book will find the chapter summaries and companion website particularly helpful.

And as a self-proclaimed technology geek, I must admit I found the interactive codes within this little book that readers with smartphones or tablets can scan for real-time stock recommendations unexpected and fun!

Anyone looking for a thorough review of the dos and don'ts of investing in low-priced stocks should add this book to their investing library. This little book goes big when it comes to empowering you to find low-priced stocks worthy of your investment dollars.

—Louis Navellier

Acknowledgments

―――――― ~ ――――――

FIRST, I WOULD LIKE TO THANK INVESTORPLACE MEDIA, publisher of my three investing newsletters, for helping me to share my investment advice with so many individual investors. I love what I do, and am thankful to the entire team of professionals who work tirelessly to ensure my timely market updates and actionable advice are able to reach investors 52 weeks a year. I am especially thankful to Melanie Russo, my publisher, and Dave Gilbert, my editor, for their assiduous effort and steadfast professionalism in our everyday endeavors. I would like to thank my colleagues, Stephen Madonna, CFA, and Robert Easter, accomplished investment professionals whose support and infectious love of the market are a source of inspiration.

Second, I would also like to recognize my professors at the Wharton School of the University of Pennsylvania, especially Dr. Jeremy Siegel. Their dynamic, out-of-the-box and creative approach to the equity markets and investing gave me the inspiration to follow my own investment theories. It was my advisors at Wharton who taught me the importance of maintaining the courage of my convictions, the most vital aspect of being a successful investor.

I would also like to thank my professors at Wellesley College, an institution that inspires women to reach for only the highest level of achievement and to be trailblazers. I must also thank the teacher that taught me the most, Sergio Orminati. I am lucky to have been his student and my ability to think and reason confidently was forever changed in his classroom.

Third, I would also like to thank my supportive friends including Rich Wilner at the *New York Post*, Saijel Kishan at Bloomberg, and Nikhil Hutheesing at *Bloomberg/Businessweek*, Scott Norvell of News Corp. and my enjoyable colleagues at the *Nightly Business Report*, Melissa Harmon and Tom Hudson. Thank you to Dr. Michael Tari of Deutsche Bank, the quantitative guru, always standing ready to help me; Peter Michael Steckmest for never letting me go, Emile Van Den Bol, as well as Jeff Blumenkrantz, Barrie Daniels and Libby Chambers, whose friendships are everlasting.

I want to thank the great Harry Clark, whose commitment to supporting his friends, colleagues, and those in need has been an inspiration for me. Regardless of the hour or the issue, Harry has always been there to provide insight and real help. Your assistance has been invaluable and your professionalism has been a model of how a life should be led. I also give my deepest appreciation to Henry Miller of Miller Buckfire, the great Wall Street legend, who has mentored me and whose door has always been open. Your time and commitment to being supportive and teaching me has been priceless. Thank you. And to my cousin, Rhea Siers, who dedicated her life to public service, has been the shoulder for me to lean on, and who brings such laughter into my life. And thank you, Cholene Espinoza, for being such an influence in my life—you're a true hero.

Fourth, I would like to thank Tim Melvin whose work on this book has been invaluable, Chris Marett for spearheading the creation of this book and Melanie Russo who shepherded it all the way to completion. I would also like to thank John Wiley & Sons for recognizing the importance of introducing investors to this unappreciated sector of the market and welcoming this little book into their series. Special thanks to Pamela van Giessen and Emilie Herman for all of your work.

And finally, and most importantly, I would like to thank my loving family. My parents, Paul and Marilyn

Kramer, gave me unconditional support; always encouraging me to follow my own path and reach for my dreams. I am so very grateful; as I have discovered that dreams do come true. And your example has taught me to enjoy life and appreciate every day.

Lt. Timothy Coyne of the NYPD—you are truly the finest in every way. Thank you for being my biggest fan and protector. And thanks to my wonderful children, Cholene and Timmy, who bring happiness and laughter into my life. Their love and presence in my heart is my inspiration each and every moment.

Introduction
The Investing Edge You Have on Wall Street

~

*Profiting from the World of
Low-Priced Stocks*

ONE OF MY VERY FIRST JOBS AFTER GRADUATING FROM college in 1986 was working as an analyst on Wall Street with Morgan Stanley. Almost immediately, I knew I found my calling. I loved every minute of investigative stock research, and quickly discovered I had a knack for finding information and ideas that others often overlooked. I advanced at a good pace, and soaked up everything

I could during that time. I developed a niche as a global analyst and was involved in bringing several companies to list in the United States as American Depositary Receipts, including such giants as BHP Billiton, the multibillion-dollar Australian mining company. And yet, one of the most memorable days for me during my time at Morgan Stanley was October 19, 1987. You may remember it from the history books as Black Monday.

I remember that day quite clearly. The Hong Kong market had sold off dramatically, so we knew walking in that Monday morning that it was going to be a tough day for the U.S. market. And it was. The U.S. market opened and slid downward like a kid zipping down a water slide. Phones were ringing off the hook and the trading floors were inundated with sell orders, causing trading volume to spike to record-breaking levels. It was very chaotic and panic was running rampant. This was the Wall Street's herd mentality at its worst.

I never was one for following the crowd, so the day after the crash while so many traders stood frozen in absolute fear, I jumped into the market, buying stocks that had been flattened during the crash. I bought as fast as I could and to the limits my funds would allow. And by year-end, the stocks I snatched up at bargain prices turned a very nice profit.

The lesson I learned that day had a profound impact on my investing career, and I went on to refine making money by investing in beaten down stocks. I managed multibillion dollar hedge funds, large portfolios for wealthy investors and achieved results so life-changing in my own accounts that I could have chosen to retire at age 37. The secret to my success over the years was that many of my biggest winning investments started out as single-digit priced stocks.

I discovered that the herd instinct of Wall Street can not only create the opportunities by pushing stocks too low, but when it reverses direction it can create incredible profits by lifting stocks out of the low-priced sector and into double, triple, and in some cases, even ten-bagger profit territory.

So why aren't more Main Street investors looking to low-priced stocks? Well, one of the biggest beliefs on Wall Street is that stocks under $10 are too dangerous for most investors. Many institutional investors, such as mutual funds and pensions, are actually prohibited from owning stocks that trade in the single digits. Stocks that have fallen below that magic $10 mark often lose the attention of the research departments, so no analysts follow them and they tend to be ignored. Wall Street often treats the single-digit priced stock sector as a graveyard, best past as quickly as possible while whistling on the way to other endeavors.

I believe that's a mistake, and one that can be used to your advantage. Any individual investor who knows how to invest on the right side of these low-priced stocks, can literally stay a step ahead of Wall Street. Their aversion to these stocks means we automatically have the best hunting grounds to ourselves.

Where We'll Go to Find These Stocks

Thanks to the devastating recession, financial crisis, and bear market of 2008, combined with the recent market sell-offs, all kinds of stocks have been dragged under $10. That means we have an unusually high number of exciting opportunities available. That's not to say there aren't dangers as well. Many stocks under $10 are cheap because they deserve to be. They are dogs that never had potential, were permanently damaged by the recession, or have misstepped so badly they have no hope of getting back on track.

That's why I've written this little book. I am going to teach you how to separate the wheat from the chaff and find those cheap stocks that have what it takes to reemerge as winners. First, I'll introduce you to what I have identified as three unique categories of low-priced stocks. With this information you can begin to assemble a list of potential investment candidates.

Some of them are what we call fallen angels. These are large company stocks that had stumbled and fallen out of favor for various reasons. Some of them were cyclical stocks where the economy had depressed business conditions and pushed down profits. Some were companies where management had made mistakes and earnings fell short of Wall Street expectations and the stock sold off sharply.

Other low-priced stocks are undiscovered growth companies. Many of these as we shall see are great companies in unattractive industries. For example, no one thinks of junkyards or waste disposal as sexy companies, but the business itself can be a source of steady gains in revenues and earnings. It may take a while for large investors to see the inner beauty of these companies, but when they do the small size of the company and relatively low valuations can cause the shares to skyrocket.

And finally, a few companies will also fall into what I like to call the good old bargain bin. These are companies that are selling for less than the value of the assets they own. Finding one of these stocks is like going to a yard sale and buying a painting for $1, only to later discover it's a Picasso worth hundreds of thousands of dollars.

Now, low-priced stocks from all sorts of sectors will surface in these three categories. But there are two sectors in particular that I want to highlight for you in this book. First, you'll find a number of low-priced winners are in medical and drug sector stocks, particularly bio-technology companies. As we age, the need for healthcare in the United States and around the world is increasing. So are breakthrough discoveries in drugs and medical devices. Many of these breakthrough technologies are the result of research efforts of small new companies and it only takes one new great drug or surgical device to send these stocks climbing quickly.

And second, finding low-priced stocks in companies that benefit from global trends is one of the fastest paths to investment success today. Around the world we are seeing nations that were once in poverty begin to grow. There is a huge need for infrastructure in these emerging economies and the companies that provide these services can do well for long periods of time. Eventually a middle class develops and companies that provide the products and services that this segment of the population clamors to own do very well. Since emerging markets are under-followed by most investors and can be quite volatile, these high growth stocks often trade at very low prices for a period of time.

How to Do the Investigative Work

Once I show you where to find these low-priced opportu-nities, I'll then show you how to roll up your sleeves and dig deep to uncover which low-priced stocks are worth your investment dollars. I've put together some simple and straightforward steps but I want to be clear: this part of the process isn't for everyone.

This book is for investors who love to dig into stocks and find out all that's right and wrong about a company. If your idea of a great weekend includes curling up with the *Wall Street Journal* you will love the information to be gained from this little book. But, if you cringe at reading the business section, this may not be your cup of tea. If you call yourself a conservative investor, this book is probably also not for you.

But do know this. I've written this book to be a fun read, with clear and simple steps to help expand your search for profitable stocks. This *Little Book* is for those who are tired of mediocre results from mutual funds and advisory services that promise the moon and deliver Toledo. My hope is that I am able to show you how to find great low-priced stocks, and that you too can reap the same types of profits I have made from buying them.

I'll be by your side not only through the pages of this book, but through a special website I've set up exclusively for readers like you. At www.bigprofitsfromsmallstocks .com you'll find additional information and how-to advice to enable you to hit the ground running once you've finished reading cover to cover. I'll point out a number of special web features throughout the book. And as a bonus to you tablet or smartphone users, you'll find a handful of interactive codes as a way to receive instant advice from me on your device.

So get ready! The journey into the world of low-priced stocks is simply one of the most exciting and rewarding journeys we can take as investors. This type of investing has been very, very good to me throughout my career and I hope this book helps you to find the same opportunities and success I have been fortunate to enjoy in this sector of the stock market.

Chapter One

The Classic Under $10 Stock

A Darling with a Record of Breakout Profits

WHEN I AM ASKED ABOUT THE PERFECT SINGLE-DIGIT stock, I like to tell the story of a company called Darling International (DAR). You could call it the classic under $10 stock. You see Darling is in a business that literally stinks; they collect the used cooking oil and grease from restaurants all over the United States as one part of their business. Another division of the company stops at slaughterhouses and butcher shops to collect hides, bones, and other animal by-products. What on earth did they do with what they collected? In a nutshell, they turned all the messy unusable stuff they picked up into useable products. This is hardly a glamorous business.

But I thought it was a very exciting business when I came across the stock back in late 2008. The stock got crushed along with everything else in the market, falling from around $16 earlier in the year. The stock kept falling, eventually bottoming at around $4 in November of 2008. The company had never been widely followed on Wall Street, but now no one cared about the company at all it seemed. But not me; I smelled opportunity and took a closer look at the company.

As near as I could determine, Darling was the only rendering and collection company that was national in scope and capability. Their competitors were small, locally-owned companies that could not compete with the economies of scale Darling was able to achieve. At the time the company had 39 facilities around the United States and 970 trucks and tractor-trailers collecting raw materials from 115,000 different locations. Most of their raw materials customers were on long-term contracts, so they had a stable supply of raw materials.

In addition to having a competitive advantage over most of its competitors Darling was not averse to simply buying them either. When I looked at the bottom line what was very clear was that by both acquisition and organic means this company was growing fairly rapidly.

Revenues at Darling had nearly doubled from $323 million in 2003 to $645 million by the end of 2007. Net profits had risen sharply as well reaching $45 million compared to about $18 million just four years earlier. The earnings per share had almost doubled from $.29 a share to $.59 at year-end. Darling had doubled its asset base over the four years and paid down their long-term debt over the same time period. The company was not slowing in 2008 either. In the first half of 2008 the company had year-over-year revenues of $422 million compared to $298 million and earnings per share of $.55, compared to only $.29 a share in 2007.

Darling may be in a stinky business, but it is one profitable company. In spite of this, by the end of 2008 the stock was solidly in the single digits, trading at $5 and change. I had to know more, so I dug into the filings and reports from the company. When I did, I quickly discovered that Darling was moving into alternative energy areas where the collected grease could be used as a source of biofuel. Now from what I saw, if the recession deepened, it was likely that the company would see some pricing pressure as demand for its end products slowed, but it was clear that the demand would not permanently be destroyed. By the end of the year the stock price slipped under $5 and it was clear to me that it was time to buy.

I didn't catch the exact low, but I was close. Darling saw some revenue declines throughout 2009 but this was more than priced into the shares at that point. Revenues declined year over year but by the fourth quarter the company was back on track and end market demand was picking up. In September of 2009 they announced a new renewable fuels venture with Valero Energy, a major oil refiner. The stock price almost doubled by the end of 2009, to around eight bucks a share. By midyear 2010 the stock price was back over $10, and it never looked back. As of July 2011, the stock is all the way back up near the pre-crisis highs for a return of over 300 percent. (See Exhibit 1.1.)

Darling International was misunderstood, underfollowed by Wall Street, and in a decidedly unpopular industry. The few analysts following the stock had too much focus on the short-term considerations of the recession's impact on the business and totally missed the big picture! Not only did Darling have a great business already in place, but its move into the renewable energy field was going to bring the company increased attention. Investors who saw the breakout potential of this company's stock could

Exhibit 1.1   Darling's Breakout Performance

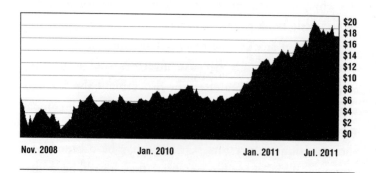

have seen short-term returns near 100 percent, and those with a longer-term perspective could hold on and more than triple their money in a little over two years.

Finding Your Darlings

In this book, my goal is to help you find your Darlings. After two decades of investing, I can tell you that low-priced stocks are a great way to build, or rebuild, your wealth. Many of my biggest winning stocks over the years started out as single-digit priced stocks. They were stocks that were off Wall Street's radar screens for a variety of reasons, but once the Street and large institutional investors discovered them, they often soared in price.

And make no mistake; that's one of the benefits of investing in stocks under $10. It's simply easier for a $10 stock to go to $15 than a $50 stock to go to $100. In fact, it's why you'll hear me refer to the best low-priced stocks in this little book as *breakout stocks*.

Breakout stocks may be excellent companies that are down in price simply because investors sold while they were selling everything else—the proverbial baby that was thrown out with the bath water. Or they may be companies engaged in dramatic turnarounds that will soon catch the attention of investors. Or they may be a brand new company with incredible potential that hasn't been discovered yet by Wall Street.

Breakout stocks can come in all kinds of shapes and sizes, but there are three things they all share:

1. Low-priced (mainly under $10).
2. Undervalued.
3. Have specific catalysts in the near future that put them on the threshold of breaking out to much higher prices.

When they do begin to break out, the snowball effect kicks in as institutions climb on board and drive the price of shares even higher. That's when we, as investors, make a lot of money.

The key, of course, is to figure out if a stock is truly a breakout stock or instead a broken stock. Wall Street would have you believe that all under $10 stocks are dogs. That is simply not the case. That means we have an exciting number of opportunities available. But there are some dangers as well. Many stocks under $10 are cheap because they deserve to be. They are dogs that never had potential, were permanently damaged by the recession, or have misstepped so badly they have no hope of getting back on track. In the pages ahead, I'll show you how to sort the wheat from the chaff.

In today's market, it is hard for individual investors to compete with all the large mutual funds and computerized investors but, as I'll show you, low-priced stocks are one segment of the market where you have a huge advantage. Shall we begin?

Breakout Tip: Keep an Eye Out

I've done my best to cram as much valuable information into this little book for you as I can. But as you read along, I want you to keep an eye out for this computer screen symbol.

That means I've posted additional information for you at a special website for readers of this book www.bigprofitsfromsmallstocks.com. This site is packed with additional tip sheets, interactive videos,

(Continued)

and even the names of a handful of stock recommendations to help you begin to build a portfolio of small stocks for big profits.

And for you smartphone or tablet users, I've even included some interactive Quick Response (QR) codes as a way for you to receive instant advice from me on your device, as you read along. They'll look something like this:

If you have a smartphone or tablet device, but have never used these codes, they're easy (and fun!) to use. See the Appendix at the back of this book for more.

And finally, I've included quick summary sections—just like the one you're reading now—at the end of each chapter for easy future referral. That way, this little book can continue to be an important reference tool for you, not just as you're reading it, but for as long as you're looking to invest in low-priced small stocks. Happy low-priced stock hunting!

Chapter Two

The Price Is Not Just Right, It's Critical

The case for under-$10 stocks

> *I do not prize the word "cheap." It is not a badge of honor. It is a symbol of despair. Cheap prices make for cheap goods; cheap goods make for cheap men; and cheap men make for a cheap country.*

BASED ON THIS QUOTE, IT SEEMS THE TWENTY-FIFTH President of the United States, William McKinley, had quite an aversion to all things cheap. Today, you'll find many folks on Wall Street, as well as Main Street, seem to have a similar, and very unnecessary, aversion to low-priced stocks.

If you were to do a search on low-priced stocks in the financial research community you would find studies that compare low-priced stocks to lottery tickets and make the corresponding assumption that the payoff chances are similar. Others focus on the fact that trading costs are higher for lower-priced issues as a percentage of capital employed and conclude that excess returns must be impossible.

The problem with these studies is that they look at single-digit priced stocks as one group without separating the companies by financials or potential. The good companies are lumped in with the bad, bankrupt, and over-hyped ones and as a result I think they reach an incorrect conclusion. It is like doing a study that concludes food is bad for you by lumping broccoli in with fast-food burgers and carrots with gravy. There are too many variables in the basket to reach a fair conclusion.

Nonetheless, the major brokerage houses seem to go to great lengths to discourage trading in low-priced stocks. Most full-service firms have much higher percentage commission rates for lower-priced stocks. Many firms, including discount brokers, have different margin regulations for stock trading under $10 to discourage speculation in these stocks. When you push the buy button on many brokerage sites for a stock under $10, you often get warnings of everything from almost certain loss of capital to an increase in your golf handicap as a result of continuing with your purchase. They attach legal disclaimers to the confirmation of the trade that are not part of the confirmation slip for higher-priced stocks.

Why? Because despite what you may have heard, price matters when it comes to trading low-priced stocks.

Comparing Apples and Kumquats

Sure it takes as much for a $50 stock to go to $70 as it does for a $5 stock to go to $7, and on the surface that almost seems to make sense. After all, in both cases it is a 40 percent increase in the stock price. All things being equal this makes sense. Where the theory breaks down is that all things are *not* equal on Wall Street. In most cases we are comparing an apple to a kumquat when we talk about a $50 stock and a $5 stock.

Let me explain. We know from basic economics that all price movement is based on supply and demand. When we are buying stock the basic unit of trade is a share of stock. Now if both companies are the same size and have the same total market capitalization and trade the same number of shares each day, then all things are indeed equal. This is rarely the case.

Let me give you an example of how this often works in the real world. Let's say that tomorrow morning 2,000 investors wake up and want to buy a bank stock. They all have $10,000 to invest in a bank stock. Half of them decide to go with Wells Fargo Bank (WFC). Wells Fargo is a very good bank and by all accounts the company did a great job of managing their way through the recent credit crisis. Most of the Street loves the stock, and even Warren Buffett is a large owner of the stock. If you want to own a bank stock there is nothing wrong with a quality choice like Wells Fargo as I write this.

The other 1,000 investors decide they will invest their cash in a breakout low-priced stock I recommended in December of 2010. Popular (POP) is one of the largest banks in Puerto Rico and has taken giant strides to improve their balance sheet and were well on their way back to being a profitable institution again. Warren Buffett didn't own any shares of the bank, but one of the most successful hedge managers of the day, John Paulson, had been buying the stock and owned a sizable position in the company.

The Wells Fargo investors would use their $10,000 each to buy 333 shares of the bank at around $30 each. In total they would purchase 333,000 shares of stock during the day. The total purchase volume would be $10 million. Wells Fargo is a $150 billion company with over $5.2 billion shares outstanding. The stock trades 37 million shares a day on average. Our 333,000 shares are less than 1 percent of the normal trading volume of the stock. There is plenty of supply to soak up our demand and our buying will result in no change in the stock price at all.

Now let's look at Popular. Our 1,000 investors will each use their $10,000 to purchase 3,333 shares at about $3 a share. The total dollar volumes will be the same $10 million, but we will buy 3.3 million shares of stock during the day. Popular is a $3 billion company that trades about 8 million shares a day. That is almost 40 percent of the daily volume of the stock and represents over 1 percent of the total market capitalization of the company. In comparison, to trade 1 percent of Wells Fargo we need to have $1.5 billion of dollar volume or about fourteen additional investors with 10 grand. (See Exhibit 2.1.) Our new demand is going to pressure the available supply and should lead to higher prices on the day.

When a low-priced stock begins to break out, this scenario plays out over not just one day, but several days if not weeks. The real fireworks start when a low-priced stock begins to gain momentum and the larger institutions begin to enter the stock. A hedge fund deciding to buy a few hundred thousand shares of a $3 billion company is going to overwhelm the supply of available shares

Exhibit 2.1   Supply versus Demand

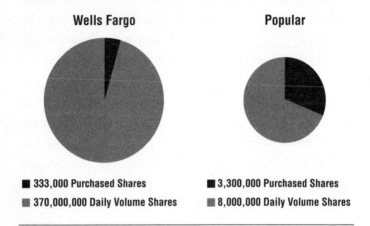

Wells Fargo	Popular
■ 333,000 Purchased Shares	■ 3,300,000 Purchased Shares
▪ 370,000,000 Daily Volume Shares	▪ 8,000,000 Daily Volume Shares

and push prices higher still. That's why the movements in these stocks can occur much more rapidly than in their higher priced cousins.

If all things were equal it would take the same fire-power to push a stock from $50 to $70 as it does from $5 to $7. On Wall Street all things are rarely, if ever, equal. The low-priced stocks we are seeking are generally much smaller in size than their larger counterparts. Even if they were once high fliers with millions of shares outstanding and have fallen on hard times, the total market capitalization will be much smaller than higher priced similar companies. It will take fewer dollars invested to overwhelm the supply of shares available and push the stock price higher to meet the new demand.

Price in Action

Let me give you an example. Dendreon (DNDN) is a biotech company that back in the middle part of the decade got Wall Street very excited about a potential new drug that was manufactured from the patient's own immune cells. This new drug represented a potentially ground-breaking step in the fight against prostate cancer. Approval of the new drug by the Food and Drug Administration appeared imminent and in their excitement to own a potential breakthrough treatment investors pushed the stock's price to over $20 a share in 2007.

They were right to be excited. Dendreon had been working on the drug, Provenge, since 2000, and the early drug trial results looked promising. And the early votes by subcommittees of the FDA seemed to indicate the drug would be approved. However, in May of 2007 the full committee met and decided they needed more trials and more information before they could approve the drug for widespread usage.

Investors did not take kindly to the news of the delay. Institutions and individuals alike exited the stock in rapid fashion. The shares began to tumble at what turned out to be the worst possible moment in market history. As we know starting later in 2007, we began to see the stock market tumble sharply in response to the credit crisis and shares of the company accelerated in their decline. The stock continued to tumble and by May of 2009 was trading at just $2.60.

Before the FDA decision was announced Dendreon had a market value of over $3 billion. After the collapse of the shares the total value of the company was less than $400 million. It was around this time I began to get interested in the company. The FDA had not said no to the drug, they had merely asked for additional trials. The early results and subcommittee votes had been very promising to say the least. So I read the financial reports of the company, as well as the publicly available FDA reports on the drug. I also checked with my sources in the biotech industry.

From my findings, it became clear to me that this drug would probably get approved at the conclusion of the new trials. That's when I began to buy the stock. I suspected Wall Street would come piling back into the stock once the additional trials were finally concluded. And with a market cap of just under $400 million, I knew the amount of money that would move into the stock would push the stock higher very quickly. I bought the stock on every down day and took advantage of other investors' fears and panic by buying as the stock moved lower in price. By the time I had my full position established in the stock, I had an overall cost of under $5 a share.

In April of 2009, the company released the full study results showing that patients taking Provenge lived longer than those on other treatments for prostate cancer. In May the FDA gave the final approval to begin producing and marketing the drug for cancer patients. As a result, Wall Street came calling in a hurry. Mutual funds and hedge funds wanted to be in on this new drug and its potential. As millions of dollars of buy orders poured in, the stock moved higher very quickly. In less than two weeks the stock was back over $20 and worth $3 billion once again. The buying frenzy continued, as it was clear the new drug would be a commercial success and a year later I sold my shares for more than $50 or a 900 percent profit. The enormous amount of money pouring into a relatively small supply of stock sent the stock straight up for over a year!

I am not going to tell you that every low-priced stock you buy in your lifetime will breakout and become a ten-bagger. Most investors only have a few of those in a lifetime. I am going to tell you that we can make Wall Street's aversion to low-priced stocks work for you more

often than not and produce consistent and exciting profits. Any ten-baggers you run across along the way will
just be icing on the cake!

Leading the Herd

When Wall Street recognizes the potential of a company
or sees that one is turning around, they come piling in
and the flood of dollars will change the supply and demand
relationship in our favor. These stocks will move very
quickly once the big funds get involved.

If we do our homework, we can make this upside
work for us. Once a stock begins to move higher, the
herd instinct of Wall Street begins to kick into gear.
While many conservative institutions prohibit owning
stocks under $10, you better believe that if a company
has discovered a new breakthrough drug, fund managers
are going to be willing to pay almost any price to own the
company. It is easier by far for them to chase a low-priced
stock that is breaking out, than try to explain to shareholders why it is not in the portfolio when everyone else is
making money in the stock. The herd instinct of Wall
Street can not only create the opportunities by pushing
stocks too low, when it reverses direction it can create
profits for us by lifting stocks out of the low priced sector
and farther than many thought possible.

Breakout Summary: Price Matters

- In most cases, comparing a $50 stock to a $5 stock is like comparing an apple to a kumquat.
- Price movement is based on supply and demand. See the Exhibit 2.1 illustration of Wells Fargo versus Popular.
- When Wall Street recognizes the potential of a company, they come piling in and the flood of dollars will change the supply and demand relationship in our favor—often very quickly.

Chapter Three

Oh, How the Mighty Have Fallen

~

Identifying Fallen Angel Stocks

IN DANTE'S INFERNO SECTION OF THE *DIVINE COMEDY*, the poet describes fallen angels as those who have fallen from grace and, although once beautiful, are now monstrous demons. That strikes me as an apt description for the class of stocks that I describe as fallen angels. These are companies that were once considered blue chip or growth darlings that have fallen monstrously out of favor with Wall Street and investors. These are stocks that were once widely owned and if not loved, at least admired and respected. Something went drastically wrong for these companies and the share price plummeted into single digits. In most cases investors sold too late and much money was lost along the way, often creating a cloud of ill will and outright distrust for these companies in many cases. To investor's eyes, these are truly stocks that are monstrous and to be avoided at all costs.

Often in the stock market, though, aversion can signal opportunity.

Fall Down, Go Boom

All too often when a stock begins to fall it becomes a self-perpetuating cycle. Investors begin to exit a stock, and then the large funds throw in the towel and sell, pushing the price below $10. At this point a lot of the more conservative institutions whose investment policies prohibit owning stocks priced below $10 are forced to sell, and the price goes lower still. Analysts from the larger brokerage firms stop covering the stock and there is a lack of new buying interest from investors. As the herd moves onto other ideas and new sweethearts, these stocks can be left to languish.

When it comes to identifying true fallen angels, there are two key questions you need to ask. The first question is *what went wrong*? Did management overdiversify the basic business and expand into areas where they had no expertise or advantage? Did the company borrow too much money and is now having a hard time generating sufficient cash flow to service their debt load? Has a competitor surpassed them in the marketplace? Has there been a change in consumers' buying habits and preferences that have left the company behind? Have there been accounting irregularities or regulatory issues that the company must put behind it in a satisfactory manner before the company can return to profitability? Are there customer or supplier lawsuits weighing on the company and its stock price? The list of problems, mistakes and management stumbles that make a once great company into a fallen angel are legion. Before you can even consider investing in a fallen angel stock you need to know exactly what went wrong and who is responsible for the problems.

The next question then becomes *can it be fixed*? Can the company shed itself of unprofitable divisions or subsidiaries that take away from the core business? Can management regain focus and catch back up to its competitors? Can the company generate sufficient cash flow to pay down its debt or can the balance sheet be restructured in a fashion that allows a return to profitability? Can regulatory issues be solved without permanent harm to the company? Can they maintain a reasonable relationship with key suppliers and customers until the current crisis has passed? Are the accounting and regulatory issues mistakes or are they fraudulent or criminal activity? Can their products and services regain acceptance from consumers? Once we figure out what has gone wrong, we need to figure out if the problems can be fixed. If so, we have a candidate for a fallen angel stock, and in my experience the companies that do achieve a turnaround can then see their stock price double or even triple before too much time passes.

It is important to understand that when you start asking these questions, you will find stocks that will turn out to be more demons than angels. Some are buggy-whip stocks, whose product and services are no longer in great demand. Some have made fatal mistakes, such as borrowing too much money. Sometimes, as in the case with Enron, there is outright fraud involved and the company is going to disappear. Companies that are going to escape from single digits and become Wall Street darlings once again are going to have to be more innovative and fight their way back to solid sales and earnings growth to see their stock price restored. The trick is figuring which will, as the poet says, have fallen but will be restored to honor.

Buy Ford Tough

One of the best examples in stock market history of a fallen angel stock is Ford Motor Company (F), an icon of American manufacturing and industry. For many decades, along with General Motors, it was considered one of the bluest of blue chips. This company was incorporated in 1903 and is widely credited with inventing the production line method of assembling vehicles. They were one of the industrial heroes of World War II, churning out vehicles to meet military demand. Ford helped create the middle class in the United States. The company went public in 1956 and was considered the perfect widows and orphans stock for decades. During boom times, Ford made billions of dollars selling cars and trucks and created enormous profits financing purchases for buyers of its vehicles.

Along the way Ford had been on something of an acquisition binge. In 1989 they bought James Bond's favorite car company, Aston Martin. In 1989 they added Jaguar to their portfolio. That same year they spent over $3 billion to buy The Associates, a Dallas-based finance company. A decade later they acquired Volvo as part of their international expansion plans. As the new century dawned, Ford bought Land Rover from BMW to add a well-known brand of high-end SUVs to their international portfolio.

As the company moved into the new century they appeared to be on track for solid growth both domestically and abroad. The redesigned Mustang was well received as the Ford F series of pickup truck dominated the U.S. pickup truck market. From 2005 to 2010 however, the company stumbled. They discontinued the best-selling Taurus line, after a 20-year run as one of the top-selling brands for government and corporate fleets. In 2005 they had to transfer $2 billion to shore up finances at Jaguar. Investors began to express concerns about legacy health care and pension costs at the automaker. Although the stock price went under double digits in 2006, it was clear to me that the company still had significant issues ahead of them. I had no interest in investing in the company at that time.

As 2006 progressed things went from bad to worse for the company. Rising healthcare costs combined with slowing sales and declining margins pushed Ford deep into the red. In all, the company lost $12.6 billion. In addition Toyota (TM) surpassed them in total U.S. vehicle sales. Later in the year Ford management made a bet that scared the market even further. They borrowed a staggering $23.6 million, pledging virtually all of the company assets to secure the loan. The new CEO of the company said that having the cash available would allow Ford to respond better to the changing marketplace and provided a cushion against a recession.

In 2008 the bottom came out from under the U.S. car market. The automakers were heavily exposed to the consumer lending market and as the credit crisis deepened default rates climbed and profits evaporated. In 2008 Ford had the worst year in its history, losing over $414 billion as the recession deepened. Auto industry executives ended up going hat in hand to Capitol Hill to plead for a federal bailout.

Here is where Ford's gamble at the end of 2006 paid off. Both Chrysler and General Motors (GM) ended up having to file bankruptcy and accept government bailouts and funding. Ford had enough cash on hand from the cash-out refinancing that they did not have to go to those lengths to survive. Because they had cash on hand they could run their day-to-day operations without government assistance. They engineered an equity-for-debt swap that reduced debt loads by more than $10 billion. Management worked out a deal with the UAW to accept stock in lieu of cash for pension and healthcare expenses. Ford's stock fell under $2 in 2009 as things looked bleak for the entire industry, and it began to divest some its noncore lines like, Jaguar, Land Rover, and Volvo.

At this point I began to get interested in the stock. It seemed to me that if Ford survived while its competitors went into bankruptcy and were dependent on government financing the stock could easily double from very low levels. Investors had a perception in 2009 that the auto business was dead. When I read the details of Ford's equity-for-debt offer, it was apparent that they could cut debt and interest payments by a huge margin and this would help the bottom line. Analysts who covered the industry told me it was very likely that debt holders were going to accept the terms of the swap offer. Friends in the auto business told me that the new models were good cars and that the F150 line of trucks was still dominant and had a loyal customer base.

It was clear to me that the company would be the survivor of the industry and that the stock was a screaming buy. Even if the recession lasted for a while the company had the cash to withstand the downturn and the new product offering would do well once consumers began to return to the car market. Cash for Clunkers helped push some consumers back in earlier than expected and the company was well on its way to recovery. Even investors who feared buying the stock under $2 could have bought the stock under $5 when it was clear that Ford could survive and would not need to follow its rivals into bankruptcy. The company has fought its way back to profitability and investors have seen their stock at least triple since then. (See Exhibit 3.1.)

What went wrong? with Ford was an easy question to answer. First, management had allowed the line of cars and trucks to grow stale. Toyota and other import companies were taking market share by offering higher quality vehicles that appealed to consumers far more

Exhibit 3.1   Ford's Breakout Performance

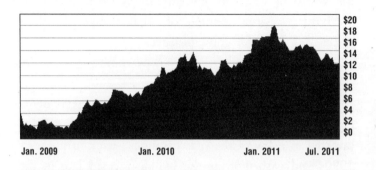

Jan. 2009	Jan. 2010	Jan. 2011	Jul. 2011

than the Big Three. Second, they restructured the business model and were highly dependent on finance profits to boost the bottom line. And third, they had expanded in a seemingly haphazard fashion, buying other auto manufacturers that were not part of their core competency.

The bigger question of *could it be fixed?* was not as easy. That question remained unanswered for me until it was clear that Ford's big bet in late 2006 was going to pay off in spades for the company. Having cash when the recession and credit crisis hit helped the company avoid bankruptcy (unlike its two major rivals) and gain needed leverage in dealing with labor unions and debt holders. It was clear that the problems not only could be fixed, but would be and the stock should go higher. Ford had made a huge bet on its future and by 2009 it became clear it was a winning wager for investors in the stock.

Ford is a great example of a fallen angel, but let's review one more for good measure.

Name Your Price

My single greatest fallen angel investment ever is one I have held for almost 8 years, and for good reason! I had invested in many of the Internet stocks back in the mid-1990s and cashed in as the bubble formed late in the decade. In the aftermath of the collapse in 2001 and 2002 I was sifting through the rubble looking at the many stocks that had crashed down to single digit prices. Many were one-hit-wonder dot-coms headed for the corporate trash heap. But not all of them; I was surprised to find Priceline.com (PCLN) in that heap, trading around $1 a share as we entered 2003. I knew the company very well from my earlier tech stock research efforts. I had even used the service and had been very pleased with the experience, as had many of my friends and business associates.

Priceline.com (PCLN) was famous for its name your own price model for travel services such as airlines, hotels, and rental cars. The stock reached an all-time high in 1999 as Internet and e-commerce stocks were all the rage. But the company began making some missteps.

They tried to expand beyond travel services using the name-your-own-price model to sell gasoline, groceries, long distance telephone plans and a host of other items. They also tried to compete with eBay (EBAY) in the online action business. For a brief time they even tried a name-your-own-rate home mortgage program. Just about all of these were money losing ventures for the company.

When the boom went bust Priceline saw its stock collapse in a spectacular fashion. From a high of $165 the shares tumbled to under $1. When I began to investigate the company I saw that unlike many of their doomed e-commerce competitors they had plenty of cash. The analyst I talked with told me they expected the company to be profitable by the end of 2003. Priceline was exiting all of their noncore operations and schemes and returning to their basic travel business. William Shatner was still on the television almost constantly in commercials for the company and I was pretty sure he was not working for free. My friends told me they were still using the service and were still very satisfied. I bought the stock in February of 2003.

Right after I bought the stock the company did a one for six reverse split to get the stock out of the dollar doldrums. This made my cost basis, or the value of my initial investment, $7.63 adjusted for splits. As I write this the stock is $543 and I still own my shares. Everything has continued to go well for the company and it has returned to its status as one of the great growth stories. I have made over 70 times my money by finding this fallen angel and asking two crucial questions: *What went wrong?* and *Can it be fixed?*

What went wrong was obvious. The stock got caught up in the collapse of the Internet boom and management tried to enter businesses where they had no competitive advantage. And once they returned to their original core focus, I felt it could be fixed and that it was only a matter of time before business and the stock price began to grow again.

Look, Listen, and Read

I do not mean to make the process of finding fallen angels sound too easy. *What went wrong?* and *Can it be fixed?* are easy questions to ask, but the answers are going to require a bit of elbow grease. First and foremost, you'll need to assemble a list of fallen angel candidates.

Your search for fallen angel stocks will often be one of the easiest low-priced stock searches. In fact, much of the time the media is going to do a lot of the work for you. When things go wrong at large companies like Ford, the financial media and newspapers will be full of chatter about the stock. Often your best fallen angel candidates will be a result of reading and paying attention to the news of the day in the markets and the economy. Stocks of the great blue chips and one-time leaders do not become laggards without a lot of attention from the media.

One way to look for fallen angels is to sit down on Saturday morning with the latest issue of *Barron's*, and if you're like me, with a cup of coffee in hand. Rather than sort through the articles or commentaries turn to the market lab section of the weekly financial paper. I look at the Charting the Market section, particularly the week's losers as well as the list of new 52-week lows. Scan the list for the names of stocks that you know pretty well. What you're looking for are the stocks that may have sold off sharply during the past week and are now in the single digits.

Another step to finding potential fallen angels is to check the stocks that make up the Standard and Poor's 500. Do a simple check to see which of these industry-leading companies are trading below $10. Remember, at this point we're merely putting together a list of possible fallen angel candidates. As I write this, just 27 of the 500 S&P stocks trade in single digits. I see former growth stock darlings like Boston Scientific (BSX) and Tellabs (TLAB) are on the list.

Finally, one of the single greatest tools you have today in your search for potential winning stocks is the web-based stock screener. It is very easy to screen for fallen angel stocks. There are lots of free screeners on the web and it takes just a few clicks of the button on any of the screeners to look for stocks with market capitalizations over $1 billion and that trade below $10. Then it is just a simple matter of looking down the list for companies that were once solid blue chips or popular growth names that have fallen by the wayside. Keep this in mind: if you are fairly active around the markets and have never heard of a company on the list, it is automatically not a fallen angel.

Once you have a list of candidates, it's time to roll up your sleeves and do the research needed to answer *What went wrong?* and *Can it be fixed?*

Your primary tools for evaluating a stock are going to be the reports each and every public company has to file with the federal government. Every quarter companies are required to file a 10Q form with the SEC that gives in-depth information of their financial condition and operations. At the end of each year there will also be an annual filing of a form called the 10K. This is a detailed review of every facet of the business, financial conditions, and marketplace for the company's products and services. All of these forms are readily available at www.sec.gov.

If you've never even seen these reports before, don't worry! I have put together a special tutorial for you at our website, so you'll know exactly what to look for:

www.bigprofitsfromsmallstocks.com. But whether you are familiar with these reports or not, please don't stop reading to dive in just yet. As I'll explain in Chapter 8, our review of 10Qs and 10Ks is not going to be your typical fare.

So for now, start gathering a list of possible candidates only. Fallen angels are the easiest cheap stocks to uncover. But please keep in mind that we are just getting started. You cannot just buy a list of large companies that have fallen below $10. Enron fit that description at one point in time, as did WorldCom and a few other one-time giants that eventually came to rest in a graveyard with a headstone emblazoned with "Worthless." At this stage, we are just building a list.

Next up, I want to introduce you to another class of low-priced breakout stocks.

Breakout Summary: Finding Fallen Angels

- Fallen angels are stocks that were once widely owned and, if not loved, at least admired and respected. Something went drastically wrong for these companies and the share price plummeted

(Continued)

into single digits. With time fallen angels return to their exalted status.

- Look for fallen angels in *Barron's* by going to the Charting the Market section and scanning the week's losers for names you recognize. Also review the current list of S&P 500 stocks for those trading under $10.
- Use a stock screener to look for stocks with market caps of $1 billion or more and that trade below $10.
- Once you have a list of stocks, ask *What went wrong?* and *Can it be fixed?* Review each company's 10Q and 10K for answers.

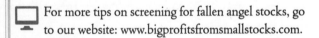 For more tips on screening for fallen angel stocks, go to our website: www.bigprofitsfromsmallstocks.com.

STOCK TO BUY NOW
Get my current **Fallen Angel** recommendation instantly

SCAN CODE ▶

Chapter Four

Growing Out of Sight

~

Finding Undiscovered Growth Stocks

NOTHING GETS A WALL STREET HEART POUNDING LIKE THE phrase *growth stock*. This term conjures up images of rapidly growing companies with new exciting products and services. There is a good reason for this. If you can find a great growth company in the early phases of its journey, you can make enormous amounts of money just by sitting still.

Much of what are commonly called growth stocks today fit into the category of what I call darling stocks. These tend to be Wall Street's favorites. They have lots of current market momentum, and tend to be heavily traded. These are the stocks you hear folks talking about around the water cooler at work. These companies tend to have cutting-edge technologies or products that everyone is excited about. (Can you say Apple?) These are not the type of stocks we are looking for when we search for low-priced stocks with breakout potential. They are already hyped, and trade at very high prices much of the time.

When looking for undiscovered growth stocks we have to think a little differently. We do not necessarily want to own the most popular exciting stocks. If everyone likes them and already owns them, they are probably pretty high in price and much of the gains are already discounted in the price. Legendary investor Sir John Templeton once pointed out that it is hard to outperform if you do what everyone else is doing. During the California Gold Rush a few miners got rich, but many more went bust. Almost all of those who went to the territory with the idea of selling supplies to the miners did very, very well for themselves. It might not have been as exciting, but it sure was profitable.

It Is Better to Be Good Than to Look Good

We are more interested in the type of stocks that legendary Peter Lynch described in his classic book *One Up On Wall Street*. Mr. Lynch described the perfect stock as one that was in a boring niche business. Preferably the company would be a business that was dull or downright disagreeable. He jokingly said that he would also like it if there were rumors of toxic waste or Mafia involvement! This type of stock would be way off the Wall Street radar screen, and few institutions would own it and analysts would not cover it or write reports for the sales force to pump the stock.

Sound familiar? We described exactly such a company as the perfect example of a low-priced breakout stock back in the first chapter. Darling International is in a business that is actually stinky. Rendering and grease collection is a dull messy business, but a necessary one. It is not one most people think about on a regular basis if at all. I have never been to a cocktail party and heard someone talking about the wonderful hide rendering company that was in their portfolio. This is exactly what made Darling such an outstanding investment opportunity. No one was paying any attention to the company as they grew into the largest company in the business and grew earnings rapidly. Darling was not only a classic under $10 breakout stock, it was also as an undiscovered growth stock.

However, mind you, not all undiscovered growth stocks are unknown. We will often find ourselves buying companies that others gave up on. In 2003, for example

Research in Motion (RIMM) saw its stock tumble. The hot technology leader in cell phones at the time was Nextel and Research in Motion was falling behind as its paging business was in the process of dying off. In addition, the company was embroiled in a myriad of lawsuits regarding patents on the various technologies it was developing. The stock price was stuck in the single digits graveyard. However in the Blackout of 2003 in New York City (where I live and work), I made an amazing discovery. The only communication device that worked was the BlackBerry. I had one and could communicate with the outside world, while friends with competing phones found that they could not get service.

As soon as the world became light again I started buying the stock. They clearly had better technology than competitors and I was very confident the stock would recover. As we know it did, the CrackBerry's success drove the stock higher by more than a hundred-fold over the next five years.

These types of opportunities unfold around us almost every day. It is research by walking around to some extent. You can see that products made by companies Wall Street is down on are actually still selling very well. When most analysts were still down on Crocs (CROX) and Heelys (HLYS) for example, I noticed that many of my friends were still wearing the ugly shoes and I was still dodging kids on high-speed tennis shoes every time I went out to the mall or the park.

Obsession Is Not Just a Perfume. It Is a Way to Find Winning Stocks

One of the best places to find misunderstood growth stocks is that class of companies that I call obsessive product companies. These companies make products that people simply do not want to live without regardless of what is going on in the economy or the world. There are some hobbies or products that become lifestyles. Many of these are not recognized on Wall Street for the simple reason that they do not share the same interests or recognize that in many cases the company in question makes a product that is not going to go away regardless of the economy. If business does slow down a bit, it is simply going to create pent-up demand. Purchases may be delayed but they will not be denied!

A fantastic example of an obsessive stock was Cabela's (CAB), the outdoor superstore company. Back in 2008, all retailers were seeing business slow down and Cabela's was no different. The markets were selling off in a steep fashion and we were entering the heart of the real estate crisis. Unemployment was beginning to climb rapidly and consumer-related stocks were leading the way down. Cabela's also owned a bank to issue credit cards to its customers, and it was expected to post loan losses in

line with other credit companies. The company had some
debt on the balance sheet and Wall Street viewed the
company as just another leveraged retailer with a credit
operation that would see losses in the years ahead. The
stock price fell right along with other retailers and the
market itself. It eventually fell below $5 in late 2008 and
stayed there into the next year.

Here is the first thing Wall Street missed: Cabela's
sells hunting and fishing products in their stores and via
catalogs, which are not hobbies for dabblers and dilet-
tantes. I may not be a hunter myself, but I have friends
who will get up before the crack of dawn to head out to
practice their sport regardless of the weather. Snow, rain,
sleet, and weather conditions' that send me heading for
the couch with a down comforter and a pot of tea does
not deter these folks. It is the same for fishermen. The
country song about a fisherman who, when given the ulti-
matum between fishing and marriage merely laments that
he's going to miss his wife is not entirely far-fetched.
Regardless of weather or market direction, hunter's hunt,
fishermen fish, and they both need the newest and best
gear to help them succeed.

Here is the rest of what Wall Street was missing:
Cabela's had over $300 million of long-term debt, but
they also had a lot of cash. At year-end 2008 they had
close to $400 million in cash and equivalents on the

books. While they had a credit card operation, the losses never really climbed the way other retailer credit card operations experienced. Sportsmen were not going to let financing for their obsessive hobbies fall into delinquent status if it could be avoided. The company had over 1.1 million credit cards and at year-end 2008 the net charge-off rate was under 3 percent.

The company was also asset rich at the time. They owned 24 of their 29 locations and the book value of the stock was above $12. The company had opened two new stores in 2008 and planned to open one more in 2009. In November of 2008, I began buying the stock under $5. Over the next year the company saw merchandising and financing revenue climb, something very few retailers experienced in 2009. Credit card charge-offs did increase, eventually reaching over 5 percent. This was nowhere near the double-digit rates that other retailers and banks experienced with their credit card operations and was quite manageable. They did open a new store in Montana during 2009 and were planning additional store locations. By year-end 2009, the cash stockpile had grown to over $500 million and Cabela's had reduced their long-term debt load. I sold the stock at $14.92 to lock in a gain of almost 200 percent in less than a year.

I wish I hadn't. Hunters kept hunting, fishermen kept fishing, and the stock today is in the mid-20s.

There will be recessions and economic slowdowns every few years. It is inevitable. It is also frequently an opportunity to find growth stocks at bargain prices and this is especially true among companies whose customers are more disciples than consumers. Obsessive lifestyle stocks are an area where investors can make money on Wall Street's tendency to rotate in and out of sectors. Stocks can be sold for reasons that are not entirely accurate and if you are ready with a list of stocks that may represent obsessive hobbies and lifestyles you can be ready to pounce when a sector sells off. Building a list of these stocks is really just a matter of observing people at play. We have covered hunting, fishing, and boating. I have friends who would golf in a thunderstorm and will skip lunch to save up for a new driver or special putter. Have you ever tried to have a conversation with an avid Harley rider without the subject of motorcycles coming up before long? I suggest building a list of these and tracking the prices every few months so you are ready to buy when they fall into single digits during one of Wall Street's mood swings.

The Unexplored Path

The search for undiscovered growth stocks often requires a different approach than Wall Street group think. While the rest of Wall Street is looking for the next new big thing, we need to look for companies that can experience earnings growth without necessarily being exciting. A prime example of this type of thinking was applied very successfully to Dole Foods (DOLE). Dole Foods has been around seemingly forever. The company was founded back in 1891 and was best known for its pineapple products for decades.

It has been part of several different companies over the years and in 2003, businessman David Murdoch bought the company from Castle and Cook. Under his leadership the company continued to expand into other lines of fruits and vegetables. In 2009 Mr. Murdoch took the company public at $12.50 a share.

Nobody cared. The stock market was still struggling with the effects of the recession and credit crisis. Growth investors were far more interested in stocks like Apple (AAPL) and Intuitive Surgical (ISRG) that sold for hundreds of dollars a share and sold sexy and exciting products. Dole had grown into the largest producer and distributor of fruits and vegetables in the world but to investors these were not exciting products. The stock price languished and early in 2010 it fell below the $10 mark where I began to take notice of the company.

I looked at the company differently. It occurred to me that the demand for healthy foods was going to grow in the years ahead. Here in the United States the new First Lady of the Land had announced that fighting childhood obesity was going to be her signature project while occupying the mansion at 1600 Pennsylvania Avenue. This was going to create attention on the need for higher consumption of fruits and vegetables, the products sold by Dole. Their kid-friendly frozen snacks and juice products would see strong sales growth as a result of new healthy eating initiatives. In the rest of the world, emerging markets were starting to create a middle class that was demanding higher quality food products and Dole was perfectly positioned to benefit from this developing trend.

Eventually investors began to realize the potential of Dole's stock price in the face of these two very powerful trends. The shares recovered from the decline and surpassed their original IPO price. As I write this, the stock is more than 50 percent higher in less than a year since it came onto my low-priced growth stock radar screen.

The mantra of most growth stock investors is bigger, better, faster. They are looking for the newest fads and the most exciting products. The truth is that the best growth stories are often found in our cupboards and refrigerators. The regular seemingly boring products we use every day can create growth stories and when those companies see their stock price fall into single digits, they become tremendous profit opportunities.

Discovering the Undiscovered

Now, while I think you'll find some terrific examples of undiscovered growth stocks secretly hiding in your day-to-day routine, I also want to share with you a more textbook approach to finding these types of stocks.

Again, I recommend you use one of the many free web-based stock screeners available to you. It does not matter which stock screener you use. Pick one you are comfortable with, or better yet use several different ones to run the same screens. I am not aware yet of any one screener that has every stock in their database. You will get lots of overlap, but from time to time you will find one or two names on one screener that did not pop up on another.

Let's begin by searching for the always-elusive low-priced steady grower. These are stocks that have been growing steadily for at least five years. Now, I want to say upfront that the output from this search is never going to be particularly wide or vast, as companies that fit the characteristics you are looking for are usually discovered by Wall Street and turn into high-priced celebrity stocks in pretty short order. However, just finding *one* of these before Wall Street does can make a huge difference in your net worth over time.

To run this search, set the screener to look for stocks that have grown earnings and revenues by at least

15 percent a year for the past five years. We also want companies that do not owe a lot of money and have decent balance sheets. Legendary investor Benjamin Graham once set that threshold as owning twice what you owe, so I think that's a reasonable threshold. Set the debt to equity ratio at a maximum of .3. This will give us a company with at least 70 percent equity and 30 percent debt as part of the total capital structure. Of course the whole point of this is to find low-price stocks, so set the maximum stock price at $10.

Your list of stocks is going to be short and the companies will be small. In fact if you ran it right now for U.S. stocks the resulting list would be just 51 names out of all the stocks listed on major exchanges and markets here in the United States. The largest company on the list is going to be just $750 million in market capitalization and the smallest is just under $30 million in total market cap. There are some pretty interesting companies and it will be worth your time to search this list and dig a little deeper to find the real winners out of this list. You want to look for companies with products that have exposure to huge potential markets like alternative energy, smartphones, and other communication devices, social networking, or any other product or service that can see continued steady growth for years to come. While we want them undiscovered we do not necessarily want them to be unknown. Some institutional ownership is a good thing, because if no one else discovers it the excitement needed to push the stock price higher may never develop. Decent levels of insider ownership are also preferable in these small, steady growers. If the founders and managers of these little growth gems still own a good share of the company, say 10 percent or more, they have a vested interest in seeing the stock price go higher over time. They are on the same side of the table as you are as investors.

The next screen we want to run is for explosive growers. These are low-priced breakout stocks that have seen a surge of earnings and revenues in the past year and are poised to break out and gain the attention of Wall Street. We usually find two types of companies on this list. One is a company that stumbled or is caught by the economic cycle and has had depressed earnings and sales. Now the cycle has swung back in their direction and they are set to surge. The other is a company that has a breakthrough with some product or service that suddenly takes the world by storm and is set to explode upward.

We want explosive growth here so we will initially set the bar high. Set your screener to look for companies with earnings growth of at least 100 percent annually. Often profit margins are also exploding so revenue growth is not as critical with this screen. Again, we do not want too much debt, but we can give these exploders a little more room, so set the debt to equity ratio ceiling at 50 percent. Of course, for all the reasons outlined earlier, we want stocks that are low priced, so set your price bar at $10 and under. At the bottom of an economic cycle, such as 2003 and most recently 2009, you will find an ever-growing list of stocks as you run this screen once a month. This will help you look at down markets as inventory-creation events and get excited, rather than depressed, when markets tumble.

We're building up quite a list of potential breakout low-priced stocks for you, and it's only Chapter 4! There are more types of low-priced stocks I want to share with you, so let's keep moving.

Breakout Summary: Finding Undiscovered Growth Stocks

- Undiscovered growth stocks are often companies that are experiencing earnings growth without necessarily being in an exciting industry. Companies whose products we use at home and at play are often the very best growth stories.
- Look for steady growers using a free web-based stock screener and screen for stocks that have

grown earnings and revenues by at least 15 percent a year for the past five years. Set the debt to equity ratio at a maximum of .3, and a maximum share price of $10. Decent levels of insider ownership are also preferable, say 10 percent or more.

- Look for explosive growers by screening for earnings growth of at least 100 percent, set the debt ceiling at 50 percent, and a maximum share price of $10.

For more tips on screening for undiscovered growth stocks go to our website:
www.bigprofitsfromsmallstocks.com.

STOCK TO BUY NOW
Get my current **Undiscovered Growth** recommendation instantly. SCAN CODE ▶

Chapter Five

Shopping the Bargain Bin

*Sorting the Treasurers
from the Trash*

HAVE YOU EVER GONE TO A YARD OR ESTATE SALE AND uncovered something you knew was worth far more than the price the seller was asking? One of Larry McMurty's best books, *Cadillac Jack*, was devoted to a bargain hunter who travelled the country looking for such bargains. Closer to home I had a friend who not too long ago was browsing a used book store and found a copy of an out-of-print book priced at $1. He paid the asking price, took it home, and immediately resold it for $1,000.

Everybody loves to buy something for less than it's worth and then resell it for a large profit. Low-priced stocks that sell for less than the value of the assets they own are one way to accomplish exactly that. We'll call these our bargain bin stocks.

Go by the Book

I do not want to get lost in a lot of Wall Street jargon, but *book value* is a term you will need to know. Book value is nothing more than what a company's net worth is. You simply add up all they own on the balance sheet and subtract anything they owe. Calculating book value is a lot like the net worth statements you may have filled out to get a mortgage loan. When we divide the net worth by the number of shares outstanding we get book value per share. Our search for stocks in the bargain bin is impossible without some knowledge of the term. We cannot tell if a stock is a bargain without a number with which to compare the price. That number is book value.

I like to make one adjustment to this number so I get a real picture of the value of the company. I subtract intangible assets like goodwill. These are clearly identified on a balance sheet when you are researching a particular company. They may or may not have value over time, but I am looking for a discount to readily saleable assets, so it's *tangible* book value. Then divide the asset value by the number of shares outstanding and we have the stock's tangible book value per share.

Bargain bin stocks sell below book value for many reasons. The company could be experiencing a slowdown in its business and Wall Street has abandoned the stock. The whole industry may be unloved, as was once the case with electric utilities stocks back in the 1980s. Cost overruns on nuclear power plants and a hostile regulatory environment had all of these stocks selling for less than their book value. In the aftermath of the Savings and Loan crisis in the early 1990s, almost all small bank and thrift stocks sold well below the value of their assets. Sometimes it is just a stock that is too small for analysts to follow and the stock price has languished as the assets have grown. Our job is to figure out if those assets can be converted to either a higher stock price or be turned into cash via a takeover or restructuring in the near future.

NIMBY (Not in My Backyard) Can Equal MIYW (Money in Your Wallet)

A great example of a bargain bin stock that sold for less than its assets and was totally misunderstood is one that comes from the refining industry. In 2008 shares of

Tesoro (TSO), a major North American refiner of petroleum products saw its stock fall well below its book value. The stock price was down in the single digits and business was, to put it kindly, awful. It always is when the economy slows down for refining stocks. Margins contract very quickly as demand for petroleum products contracts rapidly. It becomes very tough for these companies to make money. Operating profit margins for the company fell from the 8 percent level to around 3 percent and net margins fell from 4 percent to just 1 percent. To put it simply, refining is a tough business when the economy is weak.

However, when I looked into the company I found a lot of assets. Tesoro owned seven refineries in the United States. They also had 879 retail gas stations. Tesoro also owned about 900 miles of oil pipelines around the country. The big story, however, in my mind was the refineries. Refineries in the United States are pretty much irreplaceable assets. Refineries are a messy business and most people do not find them attractive. Between the not in my backyard attitude adopted by most communities and the complex regulatory environment, there has not been a significant new refinery capable of complex operations built in this country since 1977. I do not think we will see any new ones built anytime soon either. There are only about 150 refineries of any capacity in the United

States, so the large refineries, capable of breaking oil down into several different products like Tesoro's, are irreplaceable and even more valuable than they appear.

The assets already appeared pretty valuable to me. Although the business was terrible the asset pile was worth a lot of money. With the stock trading around 8 bucks or so the tangible book value of Tesoro was about $23 a share. The assets were being discounted in the marketplace by more than 65 percent. That was just the discount from the accounting value of the assets. Because refineries are irreplaceable assets the discount was even greater when you considered the real value of Tesoro's asset collection.

When I did a little digging it was apparent to me that the price action in the stock was part of a well-established pattern. I first became aware of this pattern in refiners back in 2003 when I was researching Valero Corporation, another large refiner. As the economy struggled to recover from the Internet collapse and the accompanying wealth destruction, shares of Valero fell to just $9.50 a share. As the Fed stimulated the economy conditions improved and the stock soared to $30 in just two years. Four years later as the economy continued to grow the stock was over $70 a share. The company had assets with a stated value of almost $12 a share at the time. When the economy weakened refinery stocks would sell off as margins contracted and profits shrank. At the depths of the contraction the company might even fall into the loss column. The stock would sell far below book value and large portfolio managers obsessed with quarterly performance would dump the stock. The few analysts who still covered it would advise investors to sell their shares. As soon as the economy picked up, margins and profits would climb and the stock would soar. I started buying Valero around $8 a share.

It worked that time, the same as it had every time previously. As the economy strengthened, refiners saw business improve and investors returned to the stock. Over the next two years the stock price better than tripled. Refineries have a regular pattern of falling down to the single digits and well below asset value and then rallying as the economy expands and contracts and investors who are aware of this pattern can use this knowledge as a regular source of breakout profits.

Other People's Money Can Make You Money

Asset managers, such as investment banks, fund companies, and/or brokerage firms, are another sector of the stock market that provides great opportunities to buy stocks that are cheap and trade for less than the asset value of the firm. Every time we have a bear market period investors abandon these stocks and the selling pressure often pushes them much further than makes sense given the company's assets and future earnings power when the market inevitably recovers. Back in 2003, in the aftermath of the Internet collapse, we saw the once red-hot fund companies like Janus Group (JNS) trade at a discount to asset value. As the markets returned to normal, the stock recovered from below $10 to double in less than a year.

In fact when I look in my portfolio today I see a stock that is in that business and trades at a steep value to the assets of the company. Cowen Group (COWN) is an investment bank that provides services to several different industries including hot groups such as health care, technology, and alternative energy companies. They also provide research, sales, and trading services to over 1,000 clients.

In addition to the investment banking and brokerage business Cowen is a leading provider of alternative assets offering hedge funds and funds of funds to high net worth and institutional investors. In 2009 the company had undergone a merger transaction with hedge fund manager Ramius Capital that dramatically improved their presence in this potentially high-profit sector of the financial services marketplace.

When I started investigating this company in June of 2010 what I found was a company trading at just 7 percent of its net worth or tangible book value. Investors clearly did not realize the opportunities that Cowen had lying in front of them. After briefly fleeing hedge funds in late 2008 investors were once again pouring money into alternative assets. The Ramius Funds had a very strong reputation and track record and were starting to rake in the investment dollars once again.

Cowen's alternative asset management was not its only business segment that had the opportunity for exceptional growth. It was very clear to me that we were going to see a huge increase in its merger and acquisition business going forward. Corporations were flush with cash and the best path to growth in a slow economy is to buy new assets and earnings streams. Cowen had relationships in industries like technology, defense, and aerospace that were likely to see a lot of merger activity and their fees from that business were positioned to explode. The management of the firm included Peter Cohen, the former CEO of Shearson, who had a reputation as a dealmaker, and this further increased the boutique firm's presence in the investment banking industry.

There was another aspect of the takeover business that increased my interest in the stock. With world-class management, a strong research department, and a collection of top-performing hedge funds I thought the company might be a takeover target itself. The collection of talents and assets that made up Cowen Group would command a substantial premium to book value and I was buying the stock at a fraction of book value. As I write this, all of the above is still true and I still own the stock.

Filling Your Shopping Bag

Your search for bargain bin stocks is really going to be a screen and steal mission. Like undiscovered growth stocks, these are not usually going to be the subject of much media coverage and they probably will not be the subject of cocktail party conversation either. They are cheap because they are unpopular, unloved, and something has probably gone wrong at the company to cause the share price to be so low. Most of the time they are going to be smaller companies and you will need to do a little digging to find them.

Our first tool, once again, is going to be a stock screener. You will want to look for companies that sell below book value so that should be the very first input in the screen. Set the screener to search for stocks that have a price to book value ratio of less than one. We also want to put debt classifications into the mix, as too much debt can make the most valuable assets worthless to us as shareholders. Think about a home worth $300,000 with a $500,000 mortgage. The house may have value but the owners cannot recoup the value because the loan is more than the house is worth and the bank basically owns the equity and then some. The same is true of corporate assets. Let's use the own-twice-as much-as-they-owe characteristic and set the debt to equity ratio at a maximum of .30. Naturally we want the stock price to be less than $10 to take advantage of the powerful potential of low-priced breakout stocks, so go ahead and put that as the maximum price.

Another way for assets to lose value is for losses at the company to pile up and force their sale or disposition at less than desirable prices. For that reason I usually set the screen to pick companies that are profitable. The easiest way to do this is to set the screener to pick stocks with a price to earnings ratio of at least one. If a company is losing money the PE ratio is negative and this will remove companies that are losing money.

When we look over the list of stocks priced cheap compared to their assets, we want to consider what the actual assets are. The key question is: Can they be turned into profits at some point? If the assets are cash or commodity inventories, the answer is probably yes. They can be sold, returned to shareholders, or perhaps a competitor or private equity investor will recognize the value and buy the company at a premium. Are the assets real estate, such as commercial properties, hotels, or apartments? If so they can also probably be sold at a profit at a point in the future.

The return is going to once again depend on the recent market action. There will be fewer asset-rich companies with cheap stock prices if the market has been rising and fewer if the market has been falling. Again, this helps us to think properly about stock market movements and recognize that declines are inventory creation events and provide us with opportunities to profit from potential huge breakout winners.

Breakout Summary: Finding Bargain Bin Stocks

- Bargain bin stocks are low-priced stocks that sell for less than the value of the assets they own. Buying this type of stock is like buying something for less than it's actually worth.
- Know your book value. We cannot tell if a stock is a bargain without a number with which to compare the price. Book value is nothing more than what a company's net worth is. You simply add up all they own on the balance sheet and subtract anything they owe. Calculating book value is a lot like the net worth statements you may have filled out to get a mortgage loan. When we divide

(Continued)

the net worth by the number of shares outstanding we get book value per share.

- Use a free web-based stock screener and set the screener to search for stocks that have a price to book value of less than one, have a maximum debt to equity ratio of .30, and have a share price of $10 or less. Also set a PE ratio of at least one to screen for profitable companies.

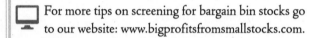 For more tips on screening for bargain bin stocks go to our website: www.bigprofitsfromsmallstocks.com.

STOCK TO BUY NOW
Get my current **Bargain Bin** recommendation instantly

SCAN CODE ▶

Chapter Six

Getting the World Healthy and Wealthy

Under-the-Radar Opportunities in Biotech

In the last few chapters, we've covered many classes of low-priced stocks, from fallen angels to undiscovered growth gems to bargain bin stocks. In each class, you're bound to find stocks from a variety of sectors. Yet when I sat down to write this book I knew I would devote an entire chapter to the biotech and pharmaceutical sector.

This particular sector is absolutely overflowing with low-priced investment opportunities—a trend I expect to continue in the near future.

There are a few key reasons for the sector's hot hand. The most obvious reason is the advancements in technology. It seems like there is a new breakthrough drug, medical treatment, or device almost every week. We have seen advances not just in biotechnology, but in robotic surgery, titanium hips, cancer protocols, and life extension programs. Increasingly we are seeing the breakthroughs come from smaller companies with smaller stock prices.

Another reason this sector is booming is the unfortunate, but very dire, need. I could go on for pages on this particular subject, but for the sake of space I'll focus on just one of the most life-threatening diseases in the world: Cancer. The statistics of this disease are staggering.

In 2010, nearly 1.6 million Americans were diagnosed with cancer, and 570,000 died from the disease, according to the American Cancer Society. That means cancer is claiming a life every minute of every day in America.

And it absolutely pains me to write that incidents of cancer are projected to dramatically increase. According to the University of Texas M.D. Anderson Cancer Center, the number of new cancer cases diagnosed annually in the United States is expected to increase by 45 percent to

2.3 million in 2030. With the flood of baby boomers turning 65 and older, the new cases are expected to occur largely among the elderly. By 2030, cancer diagnoses among the elderly alone will be roughly equal to the total number of diagnosed cases today. These are scary figures.

It is not just the United States that faces increased cancer risks either. According to GLOBOCAN, a project by the World Health Organization (WHO) developed to measure the incidence and mortality of cancer, the number of new cancer cases diagnosed globally in 2008 was 12.7 million. The WHO had previously forecast that total cancer diagnoses would reach 20 million in 2020, a growth of 57 percent over a 12-year period!

Naturally, treating these cases will require significant additional dollars on cancer spending. According to an analysis done by the National Cancer Institute, part of the National Institute of Health (NIH), total expenditures on cancer treatment will grow at least 27 percent from 2010 to 2020, advancing from $127.6 billion to $158 billion. The good news is that these treatment dollars are being funneled to innovative companies that are helping to fight the spread of this dreaded disease.

Here's where the importance of smaller, lower-priced companies in this sector comes into play. The giant drug companies are looking to partner with these smaller companies to develop new products as an addition to their own research and development efforts.

It's also worth mentioning that at this moment, big pharmaceuticals are at a bit of crossroads. Many like Johnson & Johnson, Pfizer, and Eli Lilly will see their major drugs come off patent in the next few years. That means these giants are desperately looking to fill their pipeline with new drugs. The trouble is that it takes time to develop new drugs and that's time the big pharmas simply don't have to do it themselves. That's one reason mergers and acquisitions became such a major theme in 2011. More than 40 M&A deals for more than $40 billion were announced in this sector. What the big pharmas don't have the time, and even the resources to do, they simply acquire to get it done.

And when the big pharmas are not busy with acquisitions, they are actively pursuing partnerships with smaller, more nimble players in their field. Such partnerships can produce a giant cash inflow of tens of millions of dollars to these smaller companies. A great example is the recent partnership of big-blue Merck (MRK) with small-cap Ariad Phamaceuticals (ARIA).

Signaling Potential Profits

I started buying shares of Ariad Pharmaceuticals, a small biotech company, around $8 a share in 2011. Ariad is an emerging biopharmaceutical company with three potentially game-changing cancer treatments; two are currently in clinical trials and the other expects to be accepted into trial later in 2011. The company is focusing its efforts on aggressive cancers where current therapies are inadequate using cell signaling.

Cell signaling is thought by many researchers to be a potential breakthrough in understanding and fighting cancer. Human cells, both healthy and malignant, share an elaborate system of molecular pathways that carry signals back and forth from the cell surface to the nucleus and within the cell. Such signaling communication is essential to cell functioning and viability. When disrupted or over stimulated, such pathways may trigger diseases such as cancer.

Of Ariad's three product candidates, ridaforolimus (which if you ask me deserves a better name), is the product further along the testing stage, and the one Ariad has partnered with pharmaceutical giant Merck, for development and commercialization. Merck made a $75 million upfront payment to Ariad and, after that, paid Ariad $53.5 million in milestone payments for the initiation of Phase 2 and Phase 3 clinical trials of ridaforolimus. In addition, Merck also paid 50 percent of ridaforolimus' development, manufacturing, and commercialization costs.

The deal was reworked in 2010, giving Merck exclusive license to develop, manufacture, and commercialize ridaforolimus in oncology (excluding other potential areas of treatment that may be discovered down the road). Merck now funds all development, manufacturing, and commercialization costs, and Ariad also received $50 million up front and $19 million to retroactively cover costs from January to April 2010. Ariad, of course, is eligible to receive future payments as regulatory and sales milestones are met (up to $514 million), and the company would also receive tiered double-digit royalties on eventual global sales of ridaforolimus.

The clinical trials for the drug have shown real progress. As the drug nears approval investors have gotten excited about the stock. Ariad moved quickly over the $10 level within weeks of our original purchase and, as test results are released, I expect to see it go higher still.

The partnership approach to developing drugs is going to be the model of groundbreaking research in the future. By setting up news searches and tracking the news of the largest pharmaceutical companies, you can keep on top of the exciting smaller companies that are working on potential blockbuster drugs.

Successful partnerships with larger drug companies have turned some single-digit stocks into huge winners. Regeneron (RGEN) has seen its stock price go from under $6 a share to well over $60 in just over five years as its partnership with pharmaceutical giant Sanofi-aventis has allowed it to develop promising cancer and autoimmune system drugs. Incyte's partnership with Novartis helped drive the stock price from $2 to over $20 in three years.

Smaller biotechnology companies can push the curve in new research in ways that larger more established companies simply cannot. Rather than invest in unproven drugs and technologies, the larger companies prefer to provide cash and assistance to the up-and-coming companies. In return they can access potential breakthrough drugs with less overhead. It is a win for the company, for investors in the smaller company, and often for patients. As researchers and biotech companies continue to search for the answers for mankind's medical issues these opportunities for low-priced breakout stocks will be increasingly available to attentive investors.

Ending the Invasion

The opportunities are not limited to just the drug stocks, either. Innovative aggressive companies are finding breakthroughs in medical devices and surgical techniques as well. New cardiac stents and other products are being developed, as are robotic surgical devices, bone and joint replacement products, and a host of other devices and products to improve our overall health and combat age-old problems.

I recently ran across a company that fits the bill as a potentially groundbreaking medical technology company. TranS1 (TSON), which has developed a new way of doing back surgeries that make them much better for the patient and much cheaper for the insurance companies. The technology involves back fusion surgeries, which are traditionally performed on people that suffer from degenerative disk disease (DDD). DDD can be extremely painful because a disc between two vertebrae starts breaking down, resulting in movement of the two vertebrae. During surgery, the disk is removed and replaced with a bone graft and growth material so the two disks can be fused together.

Up until now, there were two primary options for surgeons and patients. Posterior fusion surgeries require a large incision in the back, and the surgeon has to remove back muscle and nerve roots to create a pathway to the spine. Anterior fusion surgeries involve going through the abdomen to get to the spine. They provide the capability to remove more disc space and create a better fusion than posterior surgeries, but again, a large incision is required in the abdomen and organs must be moved out of the way to access the spine. Both procedures are quite invasive and require a large amount of recovery time.

With approximately 250,000 Americans undergoing spinal fusion surgery every year and extremely high costs of between $50,000 and $100,000 per surgery, this is a big business. Insurance companies want to find ways to make the procedure cheaper by reducing recovery. This is where TranS1's products come into play. TranS1's technology, which they call AxiaLIF, requires only a one-inch incision and no organs need to be moved around. Various specialized medical instruments that TranS1 manufactures and owns intellectual property rights to are required to complete the surgery. As insurance companies and patients realized the potential of this exciting, less expensive surgical option the stock shot up over 70 percent in under a year!

It Is Okay to Steal

The key to finding low-priced breakout winners in the medical and biotechnology sector is to find those companies with aggressive, innovative thinking that have the right partners. The partner may be a large pharmaceutical company investing alongside a small biotech or an insurance company working with providers to control costs and improve results. Either way it can be the path to dynamic profits that allow investors to reach their goals long before they originally thought possible.

Searching the universe of healthcare, drug, and biotechnology companies that have the potential to be explosive breakout winners takes some specialized efforts. The growth screens will occasionally turn up some ideas in this area but often it takes more digging. However, once these companies announce breakthroughs the stocks often take off very quickly. Remember how quickly Denderon recovered from under $4 back above $20? This is an area where you need to dig a little to see who may be working on promising developments.

You can find news on such developments at www.fda.gov. The site has a wealth of information of new drugs being approved and which companies are developing them. It also tracks which drugs are in short supply and could lead to production ramp-up or higher margins for their manufacturers. The site also has information and reports that will help you understand the approval process for new drugs which will prove useful over the long run as you search for cheap stocks in the medical and drug fields.

This is an area where you probably need to learn to steal ideas as well. It took me many years to develop the expertise and contacts needed to continually uncover the potential big winners, particularly in biotech stocks. You can get ideas from top managers in the field by searching through the portfolios of top mutual fund managers specializing in the medical and biotech fields. They have to disclose their portfolio to the SEC and are widely available on various research and financial sites on the Internet.

One new drug or technology can take a company from obscurity to superstardom and the stock price will go higher than you could have ever thought possible. Staying on top of which smaller single-digit stocks have promising research and strong partnerships with large drug companies can be a tremendous source of single-digit stock winners over your investing career.

Breakout Summary: Finding Biotech and Health Stocks

- The biotech and pharmaceutical sectors are overflowing with low-priced stocks.
- Smaller biotechnology companies can push the curve in new research in ways that larger more established companies simply cannot. Rather than invest in unproven drugs and technologies the larger companies prefer to provide cash and assistance to the up and coming companies. In return they can access potential breakthrough drugs with less overhead. It is a win for the company, for investors in the smaller company, and often for patients.
- You can find a wealth of information of new drugs being approved and which companies are

(Continued)

developing them at www.fda.gov. This site also tracks which drugs are in short supply and could lead to production ramp-up or higher margins for their manufacturers. You'll also find information and reports that will help you understand the approval process for new drugs which will prove useful over the long run as you search for cheap stocks in the medical and drug fields.

- You can also steal ideas from top managers in the field by searching through the portfolios of top mutual fund managers specializing in the medical and biotech fields. They have to disclose their portfolio to the SEC and are widely available on various research and financial sites on the Internet.

- Talk to your own network of pharmacists, doctors, and health care providers for the latest drug information and developments. Also look in your own medicine cabinet to see who is manufacturing the drugs you and your family are taking. You can find some great leads this way.

For additional help on your hunt for biotechs go to our website: www.bigprofitsfromsmallstocks.com.

Chapter Seven

Around the World Under $10

Investing Globally

WE SHOULD NOT LIMIT OUR SEARCH FOR POTENTIAL low-priced breakout stocks just to companies based in the United States. Foreign companies are doing more business in the United States than ever before. They are also doing business around the rest of the planet in direct competition with U.S. businesses. Fortunately for us, as the world has shrunk, foreign markets have started to behave like ours does. No longer are they the wild west of stock markets with confusing trading operations and vague accounting rules.

They also tend to trade like U.S. stocks. This means that the same cycles of fear and greed will create fallen angel stocks with the same type of spectacular potential as those here at home. Companies will be created that have exciting new products with the potential for strong long-term growth and yet stay under the radar screen for an extended period of time. We can find low-priced potential breakout stocks located all around the world in today's dynamic, connected stock markets.

The real bonus for U.S.-based investors is that many of these companies are listed here in the United States. Foreign companies can list on U.S. exchanges as American Depositary Receipts. These securities allow trustee banks to hold shares of these stocks and sell new securities to investors that allow ownership of foreign stocks. This makes trading shares of Mitsubishi UFJ (MTF), Japan's largest bank, as easy as trading shares of Citigroup.

Industrial Revolution All Over Again

Growing nations are a wonderful source of low-priced stocks. The United States is extremely developed and it is difficult to grow it further at high rates without causing runaway inflation. Markets like China and India, on the other hand, are growing very quickly and the creation of higher-paying jobs is helping to create a consumer middle class.

In a lot of ways emerging economies look a lot like the United States did back around the turn of the century. Back then people moved from the rural towns into the cities as jobs in new industries became available. Automobiles began to replace the horse and buggy. Radios and telephones became items that were desired by every household. Investing in companies that built infrastructure, like the steel and railroad companies, was hugely successful. So was putting your money into electric utilities and energy companies that served the growing demand for power. Early investors in companies that sprang up to serve these new consumers, like Sears, Roebuck and Company also did very well.

Today we are seeing similar trends developing, as smartphones and portable communications and entertainment devices are adopted throughout the world and are in high demand in emerging economies like China, Brazil, and India. Further, the robust demographic growth in emerging economies is creating the need for bigger, better, and more efficient infrastructure to maintain such growth.

Working on the Railroad

An example of the tremendous profits available from expanding our search for low-priced stocks is a Chinese railroad stock I started buying back around 2001. It was clear to me that China was going to be one of the great growth stories of the next several decades. The population of China was growing and so was their economy. The country was moving from an agrarian rural culture to a more urban industrial and high tech economy. I could see that the need for transporting goods and services around the fast-growing nation was imminent.

Guangshen Railway Company (GSH), the largest publicly-traded railroad in China, seemed to be the perfect way to invest in the growing need for transportation. Their trains serve passengers and freight lines that carry enormous amounts of traffic around China. The company operates one of the only trains that run from mainland China to Hong Kong, and their tracks connect to many of the other Chinese railways, allowing for easy transfer of passengers and cargo. As early as 2001 it was apparent to me that they had no competition in their markets and that personal travel, as well as freight loads, would be growing along with the Chinese economy.

Personal travel was the real story. Freight loads, although growing, were still just only about 10 percent of total revenues. The real story was that, for the first time, many Chinese could afford to travel to other parts of the nation to see family and friends. Younger workers in the urban areas could afford vacations and trips back home for the first time in Chinese history. As the middle class continued to develop it was clear to me that travel was going to continue to increase and this company would reap the rewards. Railroads were growth stocks back when the United States began to move from an agrarian to industrial economy and it is plain to see that the same thing is going to happen in China.

We accumulated shares of Guangshen for several years as investors continued to ignore the opportunities available in the middle-class transportation markets. As the China story continued to heat up and large investors began to get interested, the stock finally began to gain the attention it deserved. The stock itself heated up, doubling over the 18 months from mid-2003 to early 2005.

If They Come You Better Build It

When people do begin to move to cities and towns you need to have more places to live. You need roads for them to drive on, sidewalks to walk along, and countless other structures, so infrastructure and building materials companies are often in high demand.

Here's a great example: Cemex (CX). I was in Mexico back in 2001 and I noticed as I traveled to locations throughout the country that the country was experiencing a building boom. Cranes dominated many of the Mexican skylines and cement trucks and construction vehicles clogged many of the roadways. I became very curious about all this activity and I began investigating construction and building companies in the Latin American region. What I found was Cemex, a low-priced stock that served not just the Latin American regions but many other exciting markets around the planet. In addition to their home region CX sold cement in the United States, Europe, the Philippines, and the Middle East.

I already saw the building boom in Mexico and friends were telling me this was true all over Latin America and the Caribbean. In the aftermath of 9/11 the U.S. Central Bank was lowering interest rates to stabilize and stimulate the economy. This was leading to building and construction booms in many of the major markets right here at home and Cemex cement was going to be a part of much of the activity. Government spending on infrastructure, such as roads and bridges, was picking up in Eastern European markets where the company had a strong presence. The company was poised to have a strong operating performance in many of its key markets for cement products and the low stock price did not reflect the potential of the company. I started buying the stock around $8 in early 2003. Over the next three years the stock soared to over $30 and along the way I sold my shares for around $29 a share.

Interestingly, the stock collapsed again in the global recession of 2008. As global building began to collapse as credit tightened and the economy slowed, the shares fell all the way back into the single digits. In fact, Cemex stock fell below $4. Once again, as the global economy began to dig itself out, the stock slowly reversed and reached a high of $14 a share a little more than a year later.

Building materials stocks like Cemex are going to get hit hard during a time of a global slowdown, but will be among the first and fastest to recover at the first sign of an improvement in economic conditions. Emerging markets may have frequent stumbles along the way to progress but once the trend towards a more industrialized consumer society begins, history tells us it rarely reverses itself. Following building supply- and infrastructure-related stocks and buying when they are low priced and unpopular can be a path to large long-term profits.

Press 1 for Profits

It is not just building and infrastructure either. One of the key factors in initiating and sustaining global growth, especially in smaller nations, is communications technologies. There is a tremendous need to be able to communicate and exchange data with the rest of the world. In more populous and easily accessible regions of the world you can hop on a plane and take a meeting to get a deal done or exchange information. However, if you live in New Zealand, that is not always a possibility.

Back in 2001 I was looking for countries where cell phone service was still in the early stages of development. However, I wanted to look for more developed countries where there were great growth prospects for the local economy. Some of the world's less-developed nations were still in the early stages of cell phone usage, but corruption and fraud were still a large issue for many of these countries. I was familiar with New Zealand as a result of trips to this beautiful nation back when I was an investment banker working on deals in the region. Some investigation revealed that the country's cell phone structure was undeveloped, and, according to the analysts I spoke with about the nation, the economy was poised to grow.

When I started investigating Telecom New Zealand (NZT), I got really excited. The company was founded in 1987 when the then state owned enterprise bought the telephone assets of The New Zealand Post Office. In 1990 the company was sold to a subsidiary of Bell Atlantic and was listed on the Australian and New York Stock Exchanges. Over the previous decade management had invested in building the infrastructure of both the wire line and cell phone businesses. They moved into pay television in key New Zealand markets and began to offer Internet services as well. In 1992 they spent $200 million to connect fiber optic cable between their home country and Australia. When I was investigating the company back in 2001 they had just switched over to a CDMA wireless network that covered 98 percent of the populated areas of the country. They also invested in a company to give themselves a presence in the Australian 3G wireless market place.

The stock stayed around $6 a share or so for a long time. However I did not mind the sideways stock movement as the shares paid a very generous dividend. Most years I was earning over six percent in dividends alone. As wireless subscribers continued to sign on and the network grew the stock eventually caught investors' attention. In 2004 the stock really caught fire and moved steadily higher and by the end of the year the shares were over $12, more than doubling from where I first bought it. The need for increased cell phone service was obvious to me and—although it required patience—the stock paid off handsomely over time.

The same logic I used to find Telecom New Zealand has worked in other nations as well. When I looked around the Southeast Asian region, I saw that the same conditions were going to pay off as well. Philippine Long Distance (PHI) was trading in the single digits and starting to expand into cellular at the same time. The need for cellular service was probably going to be even greater, as Filipinos have emigrated and worked all over the world and want to be able to stay in touch with relatives back home. Over the past ten years, as mobile has almost replaced land line services in the island nation, the stock has been a five-bagger!

Follow the Money

When I am looking at global and emerging markets the first place I look is at the basics. Nations that are experiencing the high growth stages of their economic existence are going to spend heavily on developing infrastructure. The materials to build roads, highways, and bridges will be in high demand, as will the services of the companies who sell and use them. Money will be spent to deliver water and electricity as well as heat or cool homes. Communications technologies will be in higher demand and money will be spent to improve the telecommunications systems. Companies that build and operate these key services will prosper. The companies that supply materials or build key components of infrastructure will also do very well. If you can find them while they are still low priced before the rest of the investing world, you can reap enormous profits over relatively short periods of time.

Once we get beyond the basics of a growing country, we have to consider that all this economic activity is creating wealth. As an economy grows, people begin to earn more than they need to support their basic lifestyle and savings begin to pileup. As bank balances grow, so does the desire to improve one's lifestyle. A consumer class begins to develop that is hungry for goods and services that make life more interesting, more rewarding, and more comfortable. Companies that provide luxury items or consumer services are also well positioned to prosper as a new middle class is created in a country or region of the world.

The global markets are a great source of potential low-priced stock opportunities. By looking at developing global trends you can find those fallen angels, undiscovered growth stocks, and bargain bin favorites from all over the globe that can help you reach your investing goals.

Breakout Summary: Finding Global Stocks

- Growing nations are a wonderful source of low-priced stocks.

- Nations that are experiencing the high-growth stages of their economic existence are going to spend heavily on developing infrastructure. The materials to build roads, highways, and bridges will be in high demand, as will the services of the companies who sell and use them.

- As an economy grows people begin to earn more than they need to support their basic lifestyle and savings begin to pileup. As bank balances grow so does the desire to improve one's lifestyle. A consumer class begins to develop that is hungry for goods and services that make life more interesting, more rewarding and more comfortable. Companies that provide luxury items or consumer services are also well positioned to prosper as a new middle class is created in a country or region of the world.

Chapter Eight

Forget Everything You Thought You Knew

~

Why P/E Ratios and Growth Rates Don't Apply Here

All genuine progress results from finding new facts.

—Wheeler McMillen

I LOVE THAT QUOTE, AND IT COULDN'T BE MORE FITTING for what I'm about to ask you to do. We've spent the last several chapters talking about the types of low-priced stocks you'll find on Wall Street and where you can go to readily research those companies. In this chapter, we're going to go a step further and examine the key information you'll find during your hunt. But first, I must ask you to forget most of what you may have learned about evaluating stocks *before you ever started reading this book*.

When it comes to researching low-priced stocks, I figured out early in my career that I was going to have to forget a lot of what I thought I knew. The first theory out the window is going to be that old saw, the efficient market theory, which holds that all information is already reflected in the price of a stock. If that were true, this would all be a waste of time! When we are dealing with low-priced stocks, be they undiscovered growth stocks or fallen angels, there is no way all of the available information is already priced into the stock. For the most part these stocks are low priced because nobody is following them. Wall Street and individual stocks have sold them and moved on or never found them in the first place. No one is watching and no one really cares about the stocks. This is what gives us our edge and opportunity for huge profits.

Reading Is Fundamental and Profitable

We talked in Chapter 3 about the 10Q and 10K forms companies are required to file with the SEC that provide in-depth information of their financial condition and operations. These reports will be one of our primary research tools when evaluating potential breakout stocks.

Our review of 10Qs and 10Ks is not going to be your typical fare, either. We are looking for what Wall Street missed. We are looking for signs of improvement and plans to continue or return to a growth trajectory. For example, the price to earnings ratio (P/E ratio) isn't going to help us pick these types of stocks. After all, the P/E ratio requires the current share price and the earnings per share price for a stock. And often low-priced stocks have little to no earnings at the time they are poised to become breakout stocks, or show earnings that are cyclically depressed. Many investors have been conditioned to look for low P/E ratios, and if you're one of them, forget what you know when looking at low-priced stocks.

Ford Motor Company is a good example of this. When times are booming for the auto stocks they make a lot of money. The earnings are at the peak and are quite likely to fall in the future. In 1999, for example, Ford earned $5.86 and the average P/E ratio that year was just 9. The stock price hit a high of over $57. Neither the earnings nor stock price have been that high since. So an investor seeking a low price to earnings ratio will be all over these stocks at exactly the wrong time.

In 2002 as the economy fell into recession Ford's earnings fell to just $.15 a share. Because of the terribly depressed earnings, the average P/E ratio was an eye-popping 88.

A low price to earnings ratio-biased investor would have passed on the stock, which would have been a shame since you could buy the stock under $10 a share almost any time that year. A year later the stock had a high over $17.

Some investors have achieved success using another popular stock-picking metric, known as the price-to-growth or PEG ratio. Since this measure compares the P/E ratio to the recent earnings growth rate, it simply is not going to work for us, either. Many if not most of our stocks are coming off a fairly recent stumble of some sort and the growth rate is far below historical norms. Consider the fallen angel stock Starbucks (SBUX). Earnings had fallen off a cliff for the company and the five-year growth rate was pretty close to negative. A search or evaluation based on a PEG ratio simply would have missed this fantastic, winning stock.

As a rule we want our companies to be profitable. As we discussed, many of them stumbled and that's why they are a low-priced stock in the first place. The fact that they are still profitable in the worst of times gives us an indication management knows what they are doing and can return to higher profitability levels in short order. If they are not profitable there needs to be some reason or catalyst that we can see that will restore the bottom line to black ink in a relatively short period of time.

Better Beats Good

When we look at many of the traditional metrics used to evaluate stocks we do not use them the same way many others on Wall Street do. We are looking more for improvement or deterioration in the metrics rather than the absolute level of the various ratios and figures when evaluating stocks. Let me explain.

Let's consider return on equity for a second. This is a widely used measure in financial research that evaluates how much a company is earning relative to the amount of equity invested in the company. It is a pretty good measure of how profitably management is using the money entrusted to it by shareholders. However just the number by itself is not enough to evaluate a stock for breakout potential.

Now consider Toll Brothers (TOL) back at the end of 2006. The company had a decent year and had a return on equity (ROE) of 20 percent. Now, by anyone's scale, 20 percent is a pretty good return and indicates that management is doing a decent job of managing shareholders' capital. If we just looked at the numbers in a static manner we might have been impressed. However, on a comparative basis, the number had a huge flaw. Year over year the ratio had dropped by almost 33 percent compared to the prior year. The return on shareholders' investment was declining and this was a huge red flag in my eyes. We all know what happened next. The housing market imploded and profits continued to shrink to the point Toll squeezed out a small ROE in 2007 and was deeply in the loss column by 2008. Instead of an absolute number we want to pay attention to the *direction* of the numbers.

Think Different, Do Better

Researching low-priced stocks to find potential breakout winners requires a different thought process than you may have learned about in the past. Mainstream research tends to be, well, mainstream. We do not pick the same old stocks in the same old way. That would give us the same old results and that is *not* what we want to accomplish. We are looking for stocks that can breakout in a big way and show profits of several times our purchase price.

Breakout Summary: Looking for What Wall Street Missed

- Your primary tools for evaluating a stock are going to be the reports each and every public company has to file with the federal government. Every quarter companies are required to file a 10Q with the SEC that gives in-depth information about

---

their financial condition and operations. At the end of each year there will also be an annual filing of a form called the 10K. 10Q and 10K reports can be found at www.sec.gov. If you've never even seen these reports before, don't worry! I've put together a special tutorial for you at our website www.bigprofitsfromsmallstocks.com.

- Traditional Wall Street research does not work for finding low-priced breakout stocks!
- If you've been conditioned to look for low P/E ratios, forget what you know when looking at low-priced stocks. The P/E ratio requires the current share price and the earnings per share price for a stock. And often low-priced stocks have little to no earnings at the time they are poised to become breakout stocks, or show earnings that are cyclically depressed.
- Don't look to PEG ratios either. Since this measure compares the P/E ratio to the recent earnings growth rate it simply is not going to work for us.
- Also, return on equity (ROE) by itself won't help us pick stocks. We are looking for directional trends rather than actual numbers.

Chapter Nine

Looking for the Right Stuff

~

Survey These People, Places, and Things

ONE OF THE KEY THINGS WE WANT TO EVALUATE WHEN we are looking at a low-priced company is the strength of the balance sheet. In general terms we like to stick with the old adage of owning at least as much as you owe. With that in mind, we want the majority of our companies to have a debt-to-total-capitalization ratio of 50 percent or less. All this means is that we add up the equity portion of the balance sheet with the debt and want the debt to be one half of the total. This gives us a financial situation where bankruptcy or other forms of impairment are far less likely to occur when we own the stock.

I also like to get a lay of the land by looking at operating leverage. This is simply a measurement of how much an additional new dollar of revenue impacts earnings. Companies that have high fixed expenses or capital requirements can be said to have very high operating leverage. Sprint (S) is a great example of a company that has high operating leverage. They had already spent the money to upgrade their network and expand into 4G coverage across a wide swath of the United States. The money was already committed and being spent out of existing cash and financing sources. Every new customer Sprint is able to sign up sees the lion's share of the monthly bill go right to the bottom line.

When I am looking over the balance sheet of potential stocks I like to keep in mind a saying we have around the office: *Every asset is eventually an expense*. When I look at a company's assets I like to consider what they are and what expenses they may eventually generate. Buildings need repairs at some point in time. Computer networks need upgrading. Inventories need to be replaced. Machinery breaks down and becomes out of date. As I look through the statements and management's discussion sections of a 10Q or 10K I check to see when the last upgrade or replacement cycle was completed. If it has been a while there could be higher expenses and lower profits on the horizon.

It is also very important to read the footnotes and fine print in a filing of a prospective stock. I want to see if the auditors signed off and issued an unqualified opinion of the company's financials. If they issued a qualified opinion that's a huge red flag that something may be wrong with the data I am using to evaluate the company. Has the company recently changed auditors? That can be a flag as well, and indicates the previous firm had some questions the company didn't want to answer or did not like the conclusions the auditor drew out of the financial data. Is there a concern about the company's ability to continue as a going concern? Are there a lot of complex off-balance-sheet arrangements? These could have a substantial negative influence on the company's leverage and operating ratios that are not included in the basic balance sheet and income statement presentation.

Now Presenting . . .

Once we have dug through the basic filings let me introduce you to one of the best tools you have for accessing information when evaluating a stock. Just about every company has an investor relations section on their corporate website, which includes press releases the company has issued during the past few years, as well as a listing of which Wall Street firms provide analyst coverage. Most investor relations sections also have links to SEC filings and financial information about the company.

I will use one of my former stock holdings, Wendy's/ Arby's Group (WEN), to give you an idea of how valuable this tool can be. When I go to the investor relations section of their website I find links to all their SEC filings, historical information about their finances, and stock price. The last few years of press releases, including quarterly earnings reports, are readily available. The really interesting section to me is webcasts and presentations. Here I find links to recent presentations at various conferences and investor meetings, including videos and PowerPoint presentations.

I see in this section that Wendy's management recently gave a presentation at a growth stock conference for investors organized by a major brokerage firm's research department. Now I am a little cynical when I read these presentations as I am aware that management is putting their best foot forward. However with today's strict securities laws I am not too concerned that they will stray too far from the truth of the matter, so this is a valuable source of information on management's outlooks and plans for the company.

I see from the presentation that the company is introducing a new line of burger products in the second half of 2011 that look pretty enticing. They have a strong balance sheet and are buying back stock. I see in the presentation that they have recently increased the dividend. Management is continuing with their efforts to sell the Arbys' business and refocus on the core Wendy's brand. The presentation contains information about international expansion plans, menu changes, as well as a discussion of finances. This is all valuable information and reinforced my conviction about owning the company.

Not all companies have these in-depth presentations on their investor relations section, but many do. Once you do the initial reading and digging through the SEC filings, the company's website should be the next place you head. Make use of the very valuable information the company is providing.

Pictures and People

The next thing I like to do is look at the stock price chart. I am not a chartist by any means, but the price chart can provide valuable information, especially in timing my purchase of a low-priced breakout stock. Is the stock moving higher on increased buying activity in the stock? This could be a sign that the larger investors, such as hedge funds, are starting to notice the company and I want to get in as soon as possible. Is the stock breaking out to new highs? Has it bounced off a level of support, such as a double price bottom that might indicate institutional buying is putting a bottom in the stock and the time to buy has been reached? I never make a decision because of the chart itself but if the stock has passed the research process, charts can provide valuable information about what other investors think of the company.

Another important piece of information I like to check when evaluating a stock is who is buying and selling the shares. Are insiders buying or selling the stock? If they are selling is it just one officer or director or several of them? One seller could be someone in need of cash for some personal reason but many sellers over a period of time is a huge red flag. If the folks running the company are selling, I am not so sure I should be buying the stock. I need to check my conclusion. Insiders may sell for several reasons, but they only buy for one: They like the potential of the company and think the stock is underpriced relative to the potential for gains in the future. Insider buying increases my conviction about a company that has passed all my other tests.

I also take a look at what other funds or large investors are buying. This information is readily available to sites like NASDAQ Stock Quotes or GuruFocus.com.

I do not own the only pencil and calculator on Wall Street and I like to see that at least a few other smart investors have expressed interest in the stock. These hands-on shareholders are often a catalyst in themselves, as they push management to create change and unlock shareholder value.

Impartial Opinions

I also make a lot of phone calls when I'm researching a company. I call Wall Street analysts who cover the stocks I am investigating, and I call on my network of experts. Over the years I have cultivated a network of people who are knowledgeable in a wide range of fields from technology to medicine and just about everything in between. During my 25 years on Wall Street, I got to know analysts covering every field from just about every firm in the business. This network is invaluable when it comes to digging deeper on potential low-priced breakout stocks.

Let's start with the analysts. I talk to them all the time and they have given me some insights and financial information along the way. The truth is the information they give me is available in other places and it is readily available to you if you know where to look. You may even be able to gain an advantage as the analyst calling me has something to sell and tends to push stocks their firm has a relationship with or favors for some reason. You can access some more sources that are potentially less biased.

There are some great research resources available to you. One of the oldest and best is Value Line, the venerable research publication. Investment luminaries like Warren Buffett and Peter Lynch are among those who have praised the advisory service. Value Line has been around since 1931 so it has stood the test of time. In addition to its momentum-based proprietary ranking services, the weekly publication provides more than a decade's worth of historical financial data that allows you to quickly spot changes and trend in corporate fortunes or misfortunes. They also provide analyst commentary that may give you insights into a company's potential to be a winning stock.

Standard and Poor's also publishes valuable stock research that is easily available to investors. Many of the discount brokerages, including leading firms like Charles Schwab and Scott Trade, offer this research as a free benefit for customers. A lot of Morningstar's equity research, including historical financials and ratios, is available free on their website. Sites like Yahoo! Finance give you one click access to analyst estimates and opinions on their site as well. The wealth of information available on the web allows you to gain access to almost all of the same opinions and information as I get from analyst sales calls. As a bonus you won't have to sit through some of the long, boring presentations I have had to attend over the years.

It Is the Network

What about the network of experts in various fields? It is true I consider this one of my most valuable resources in evaluating stocks and unearthing hard-to-find information. It is probably not true that you do not have access to information about new technologies, products, and services within your *own* network. Most people have a network available to them but they just do not use it properly.

Let's walk through a weekend together and see what network and information opportunities we can uncover. Start with Friday afternoon as the work week winds down. You finish up in the office, turn off the computer, grab a few files you need to review and head out the door. As always you look forward to meeting the gang for Happy Hour at your favorite spot. You dash down to the garage, hop in the car, and head to your gathering spot for Friday libation and conversation to kick off the weekend. As you stroll into the inviting local bar you see the whole gang is there ahead of you. Linda is there with a frosty cosmopolitan in front of her as always. She is an account executive at a regional advertising firm and is on the fast track in the industry. Sue runs the call center for a credit card company and is at the corner table, with her husband Sam, with some umbrella drinks in front of them. They have been talking about a trip to an island resort as soon as Sam makes regional manager at the mobile phone store chain he has worked for the past five years.

You are glad to see that Betsy made the weekend gathering. She is a pharmaceutical rep and their latest product launch has kept her busy the past few weeks and you have not seen her in a while. It will be nice to catch up with her. Joe is there, but then you can't remember the last time he missed a Friday get together. As always he will be leaving early since the car dealership he manages opens early on Saturday to take advantage of weekend traffic. Louise pops in declaring loudly that she needs a drink pronto. It has been a busy week for her as she is helping a new client locate a suitable office building to lease. After an hour or two of pleasant chatter you head off to home where your spouse and kids are looking forward to a great weekend together.

The next day it is up and out early to the local little league field. Your son has a big game today. As the kids take the field you are chatting on the sideline with one of the other parents. Dr. Johnson is a leading oncologist in town but he always makes time to see his star third baseman son handle the hot corner! The coach is also the sponsor of the team. In fact, Paul Smith's sporting goods store has been sponsoring little league teams around here for as long as you can recall. You see Mary arrive with her flock and head over to chat. Mary is the manager of a local branch of a national bank and your kids have been friends since they were in diapers. After a come-from-behind victory it's time to gather the kids and head home for weekend chores and some family time.

It is not even noon on Saturday and look at the opportunities you have had to gather information. Linda probably knows all about advertising tends and corporate spending patterns. She may also know what products are red hot in the market right now that her customers sell. There is probably not much Linda does not know about credit card spending levels and trends in defaults. Sam is almost sure to know which smartphones are red hot and which ones are definite duds. Louise knows volumes about which drugs are gaining physician acceptance and what the upcoming hot new drugs might be. I would venture a guess there is not much Joe does not know about his and his competitors' cars. I promise you he is aware which ones are flying off the lots and which ones are gathering dust.

Dr. Johnson is up to date on all the leading cancer treatments and has read of potential breakthrough drugs. Mary knows all about conditions in the banking business and probably has a lot of information about trends in the economy as well. Paul Smith knows which new drivers are considered mandatory additions to the bag and which ones are flops with the weekend duffers in your town. Your town is like a lot of other towns, so the information can give you a clue about those golf-related companies that may prosper.

People, Places, and Things

The lesson here is to get talking, get researching, and get to it! You may not be aware of it, but you probably have the resources and network to help you explore under-the-radar stocks. Of course, if you need a little more of a nudge, stop by my *Little Book* website (www.bigprofits fromsmallstocks.com) for more information on how to go looking for the right stuff.

Breakout Summary: Looking for the Right Stuff

- We look for companies that own at least as much as they owe. We want to have a debt-to-total-capitalization ratio of 50 percent or less. We also look for a high degree of operating leverage.
- Check the fine print of those 10Qs and 10Ks. If the auditors issued a qualified opinion, that's a

huge red flag that something may be wrong with the data used to evaluate the company.

- Use the investor relations section of a company's website. Just about every company has such a section at their corporate website. There's a host of helpful information there.
- Find out who is buying and selling the stock—from insiders, to funds, or large institutions. Insiders may sell for several reasons but they only buy for one. They like the potential of the company and think the stock is underpriced relative to the potential for gains in the future. Insider buying increases your conviction about a company that has passed all your other tests.
- Research what the analysts are saying. There are some great research resources available to you. One of the oldest and best is Value Line. Standard and Poor's also publishes valuable stock research that is easily available to investors. Many discount brokers offer this research as a free benefit for customers. Yahoo!'s finance section also gives you free access to analyst estimates and opinions.
- Explore you own network of contacts! Most people have a network available to them but just do not use it properly.

For additional help finding the right stuff go to our website: www.bigprofitsfromsmallstocks.com.

Chapter Ten

Well Bought is Half Sold

—❧—

Knowing When to Sell in Good Times and Bad

ONE OF THE HARDEST PARTS ABOUT INVESTING IN ANY type of stock is knowing when to sell. Fortunately for us when we are dealing with smaller stocks, a stock bought right is half sold. By focusing on lower-priced stocks a lot of our selling decisions will be made for us by the market itself. I will come back to this very important point later in the chapter but first I want to deal with the other, perhaps less pleasant, side of selling stocks.

As much as any of us may hate to admit it there will be times when after doing all the work and enjoying the excitement that comes with finding a great potential winner, it is just no fun to admit that perhaps our analysis was wrong or the facts have changed and we have to sell the stock. Often this will incur a loss and nobody likes a losing stock position. No golfer shoots par every time out and no stock picker has all winning stocks. Selling stocks that do not work out in our favor is just another part of the investment process and we need to learn how to deal with that fact and take action when needed.

Ask Yourself This

When you start investing in low-priced breakout stocks it is necessary to monitor your portfolio on an ongoing basis. While it's always nice to see the winners in the portfolio, always start with the stocks that are not doing so well right now. When a stock moves against you, see what you missed in my original analysis. Here's the key question to ask yourself with every stock that is down in price: *Are you wrong or are you just early?* Did you miss a key factor or has something changed with the company that materially alters your original thoughts on the stock?

You want to read any filings or news releases since you bought the stock. Has the company taken on more debt? Did they miss a key product launch date? Is the company spending its cash at an alarming rate? Are inventories growing as customers delay or cancel orders? Have regulatory or legal issues emerged that change the outlook for the company? Have the macroeconomic issues that face the company changed since you bought the stock? You are looking for material negative changes in the company or its outlook since you originally bought the stock. If there are any, then you want to sell the stock. The old adage that the first loss is the best one holds true. If the situation worsens, do not wait for a bounce or to get back to even—sell the stock and move on.

You also want to watch what insiders are doing with their stock. If they are buying that is great. If one or two insiders are selling relatively small amounts of stock that's usually a non-event; they could be raising cash for anything from estate-planning concerns or a new boat. However, if there is a pattern of regular consistent selling by many insiders in a stock that has moved down in price, you want to know why they are selling. Has the stock gone too far too fast? Perhaps they are seeing signs that business will slow in the near future. If there is persistent large selling by officers and directors you want to challenge your original conclusions. You might have missed something important and need to sell the stock right away.

Often the stock still fits the profile of a potential breakout stock and you might even consider buying more shares to lower your cost in the stock. Let me give you a prime example of the review and selling process with some recent decisions I made in my portfolio in June of 2011 to help you understand the process you will want to do with your portfolio of breakout stocks. When I looked at my portfolio I had some positions that were down in price. Several of them were small bank stocks that I purchased anticipating a turnaround in the banking business. When I reviewed the company financials and news it seemed clear that my original conclusions were still very much correct. The little banks I owned were turning the corner. They were starting to show profits and loan losses were slowing as the credit crisis began to ebb somewhat. Conditions were not perfect but they were actually a lot better than when I originally bought the shares. I was early and Wall Street's extreme pessimism was weighing on the shares, but the long-term outlook for small banks was still good. There was no need to consider selling these stocks.

But one company did have some material changes. I originally purchased L&L Energy (LLEN) because it appeared the company was in a great position for the

looming shortage of coal in China. LLEN operates profitable coal mines, coal wholesale, coking, and coal-washing
facilities in the Yunnan and Guizhou Provinces. China's
galloping economy now uses half the six billion tons of
coal used globally each year and the government was
expressing concerns that supplies would run tight. This
would be great for LLEN, as tight supplies led to higher
prices.

Something had indeed changed. L&L Energy was a
reverse merger company (when a private company
becomes public by purchasing control of the public company) and the accuracy of the financial statements and
earnings of these one-time shell companies were being
challenged by analysts. Management at L&L had done
little to clear up concerns about their financials and it
was hurting the stock price. No matter how good the
prospects of the coal mines might be, a lack of clarity
in financial statements was a serious concern. It was
unacceptable to continue to own shares in a company
where it was unclear how much they actually owned,
owed, or made. So, I sold the shares and took the loss.
I may not have been happy about it, but it was the right
thing to do.

The important thing when selling a position that did
not work out is going to be your attitude. It is simply
part of the investing process. As long as the majority of

your low-priced picks turn into breakouts you will still make plenty of money. Letting a loss challenge your thought process or ego will have devastating consequences on your long-term results. Things changed so you changed your opinion, which is the smart and correct way to approach the sale of a stock that did not work.

We Have a Winner

Now let's move on to those happier selling occasions. As an investor nothing is as satisfying as ringing the bell and cashing a profit. The hard part for many is figuring out when to sell a stock that has risen in price and has gains. Again, the answer lies in constant review and reading of the news and financial statements being released by the company. When you are done checking out the stocks that are down in your portfolio you want to take a look at the fundamentals and news from your winners and make sure you think they can still breakout higher and deserve a place in your portfolio.

There are several key barometers you can use to check your stocks. The first one is pretty obvious. Since we are focusing on single-digit stocks to reach our goals, when a stock price crosses $10 you want to sit down and review the situation and see what's happening with the company and the stock price. Are revenues and profits still growing or rebounding? Is the company paying down debt and fixing any balance sheet issues they have. Are new products being well received in the marketplace?

On the technical side of things, is daily trading volume increasing or at least staying steady? This can be a sign that the big institutions that sold the stock when it was falling are now buying back in and this is going to push the stock price still higher. Is the stock making new 52-week highs? Are you seeing a steady pattern of higher highs and, more importantly, higher short-term lows in the stock? Stocks are always going to move in ebbs and flows. When you chart a low point of a pullback above the low point of the prior round of profit taking, this is a very bullish sign for the stock. Buyers are moving in and the stock is probably heading higher, so ride the wave and let your profits grow.

As long as things are improving you want to own the stock. I have stocks today like Priceline that I have simply never sold even though they have risen by hundreds of percent. The business keeps getting better and buyers are still enthusiastic about the stocks. I may have paid a low price for them but as long as things improve, I am comfortable holding these stocks as they go higher.

As stocks move higher there are some indications that indicate it is time to part ways with the stock. If business starts to slow and is no longer improving it is time to sell. If revenues and earnings have been rising and then the company announces a down quarter, it is time to ring the register and take your profits. If you have a stock that has moved higher and the company announces a large debt or equity offering, you want to consider selling the shares. The offering is going to put weight on the stock and it is going to pull back. If it comes back down to a level near your entry you can consider buying back the shares. The need to raise money is a sign that the company is not generating enough cash to meet its goal and it's a reason to consider taking profits.

As a stock moves higher it's often a good idea to scale out of the position. If you are a somewhat more conservative investor it's a great idea to sell some of your position when a stock has doubled in price. Now you have your original investment back and are, as they say in Vegas, "playing with house money" and can buy another low priced stock. Even if you still like the stock there is something very comforting about knowing you no longer have any of your original capital at risk.

Love and Hate

One other important sell signal is that all of a sudden everyone else loves what they once hated when you were buying. Odds are when you were originally buying a low-priced breakout stock, no one had heard of it or everyone hated the stock. All of the research reports that were downgrading the stock and advising you to sell, are now giving enthusiastic upgrades and buy suggestions now. The talking heads now love the stock and are talking about the marvelous turnaround and bright prospects ahead for the company. As Warren Buffett once observed, you pay a high price for a cheery consensus on Wall Street. If everybody loves it, the question becomes who is left to buy it? We are buying undiscovered, unloved stock and when they are well known and well loved it is probably time to sell them.

If you have an undiscovered growth stock that is added to one of the popular indexes, it is definitely time to consider selling. You will get a pop in price after the announcement of index inclusion is made and much of the time you want to consider selling right there. The underperformance of stock added to an index is pretty well documented in academic circles. You also have a whole new set of circumstances to deal with and will be subject to the influences of index and short-term traders.

Growing, Growing, Gone!

My absolute favorite way to sell a stock is because I have no choice in the matter. When we are buying single-digit breakout stocks we are buying companies whose prices and market capitalizations are very low. While other investors may not be taking notice, there is another group of folks who are paying very close attention to low-priced stocks looking for bargains. Chief executive officers and chief financial officers of other companies in the industry are paying very close attention to these stocks. So are the very astute folks at private equity firms and leveraged-buyout shops.

In the corporate world growth is the mantra of the day. If you are not growing shareholders will be angry with you and, often, activist investors will begin to exert pressure on the company. The problem many companies face is that growth can be expensive to achieve. The cost of opening new locations or developing new products can be extremely expensive and be a drag on earnings. That's the last thing you want to see happen. There is another option available to larger companies. If there is a smaller company out there that has attractive locations offering similar products, or has services that would be a good fit for your company, you can just buy them and gain instant growth. When an industry is experiencing difficult times, astute executives will move to buy low-priced competitors to take advantage of the inevitable cyclical rebound in the industry. As we discussed in Chapter 6, drug companies are constantly looking for smaller companies with new products to expand their product lines and they often achieve this by investing in or acquiring smaller companies.

Private equity firms are always on the prowl for undervalued assets and earnings streams they can buy. These firms use leverage to buy companies and then run them for several years. The idea is to improve operating performance, pay the debt back down, and then resell them to the public at much higher prices. They are looking for mispriced assets that can be acquired cheaply or companies who can grow at accelerated rates for years to come and have not been driven higher by Wall Street.

The stocks in your portfolio of potential single-digit breakout are perfect candidates for acquisition by either type of buyer. We are looking for companies that have great growth rates or cheap assets and can be purchased for small amounts of money. So are both types of potential buyers! As you progress in your career as a low-priced stock investor you will end up selling many stocks because you simply have no choice. A corporation or financial buyer will come along and buy the entire company and you will have no choice but to sell. The good news is that to get that deal done buyers have to pay a premium to the current market price and this means profits for you!

So remember, a stock bought right is half sold, but sometimes stuff happens. The myth of the one-decision stock has been proven false countless times over the years. When we are buying unloved and unknown stocks they will eventually be discovered and find themselves back in favor on Wall Street. This is the very cycle of fear and greed we want to exploit for our gains. "When the dogs are hungry feed them" is a saying that used to circulate around Wall Street trading desks back when I first started. If investors are hungry for something you own and willing to pay for it, let them have it!

Breakout Summary: Knowing When to Sell

- Keep a close eye on your low-priced stocks. When a stock moves down, you must answer the following question with brutal honesty: Was I wrong or am I just early?
- Letting a loss challenge your thought process or ego will have a devastating impact on your long-term results.
- As long as things are improving, it's okay to own the stock. If business starts to slow and is no longer improving it is time to sell.
- As a stock climbs higher, it's often a good idea to scale out of a stock. If you are a somewhat more conservative investor, it's a great idea to sell some of your position when a stock has doubled in price.

- My favorite reason to sell a stock is because it's been acquired. To close the deal buyers have to pay a premium to the current market price and this means profits for you!

For more tips on knowing when to sell go to our website: www.bigprofitsfromsmallstocks.com.

Chapter Eleven

Beware the Wolves of Wall Street

~

*Practical Advice on Your
Journey to Profits*

ONE OF THE THINGS THAT MAKE LOW-PRICED STOCKS such a fertile hunting ground is Wall Street's aversion to single-digit stock prices. Many brokerage firms have higher fees and margin rates on lower-priced stocks, and others still will not allow trading in them at all. There is a general mindset that low-priced stocks are riskier than their higher-priced brethren. I just do not think that is so. If you take a $30 stock and a $5 stock where the companies have similar financial characteristics, the risk is pretty much the same in my eyes. A low-priced stock with high-priced quality financials is less risky than a higher-priced issue. All things being equal, the answers to the risk versus reward equation are found in the financial statements, not in the stock price. This is a classic case of broad-based statements, such as "all low-priced stocks are risky," just being wrong. However, that wrong conclusion is what creates many of the opportunities for us to make money exploiting others' wrong conclusions.

There are some things we need to consider when dealing with low priced stocks. I would be remiss if I did not address some of the special risks and factors involved in the trading of lower-priced stock issues. Some of these risks are perceived and a few are technical issues you need to be aware of as you search for low-priced breakout stocks.

Avoid the Bad Guys

This segment of the market has always been susceptible to special risks, including fraudulent schemes to sell worthless stock to unsuspecting investors and artificially manipulate the prices of some issues. Movies such as *Boiler Room* and books like *The Wolf of Wall*

Street illustrate some of the unethical and downright criminal behavior that occurs in low-priced stock issues. The manipulation of low-priced stocks was so widespread that the criminal activity actually appeared on an episode of *The Sopranos*!

The schemes are all some variation of what's called a pump and dump. Unscrupulous operators accumulate or create a large block of stock at a very low price. They then hype the stock as the next big thing to unsuspecting investors. They talk about getting in on the ground floor, revolutionary breakthroughs, and other buzzwords designed to get the blood pumping and the greed flowing. When investors get excited about this wonderful company, the operators simply dump their stock at much higher prices and walk away with investors' hard-earned money.

Most of the time these companies have no real business or assets. They are just shell companies set up for the specific purpose of fleecing investors. Some of them may be little mining stocks or small tech companies that are badly underfunded and will be broke and bankrupt very shortly. The only winners in these schemes are the crooks that peddle the stock. The best way to avoid getting caught up in this type of fraud is to avoid the come-ons and advertisements for companies you have never heard of, or are recommended by someone you have also never heard of.

The SEC has done a great job of cleaning up the penny stock brokerage firms and they are not as prevalent as they once were. However there are still a few out there and as long as greed and dishonesty exist there always will be. Escaping their clutches is pretty easy. If you get a phone call from a broker you do not know pitching a low-priced issue, just hang up. When you go to the mailbox and find a fancy investment pitch promising untold riches in some new revolutionary company, throw it in the trash.

Again there is good news amongst the bad. Popular culture feeds off Wall Street's aversion to low-priced stocks to make things seem far worse than they actually are in reality. Movies like *Boiler Room* help feed investors aversion to low-priced stocks. As I like to say when dining with someone on a diet, "More cake for me!"

On the Internet, No One Knows You Are a Dog

Most of these stock hype promotions today will come to you via the Internet. It seems like there is some new penny stock promotion in my inbox just about every day. The criminals have simply moved from the regulated world of brokerage firms to the faceless anonymous Internet to perpetuate their schemes. The same rules for avoiding their clutches apply. If you are getting promotions from some one you never heard of or some distinguished-sounding research firm providing information on wonderful opportunities to make millions of dollars off the next big thing, just hit delete. If you do not know them or never heard of the company, 99 percent of the time the delete button works just fine. If you are spending time on some of the web-based bulletin boards devoted to the stock market and someone is making unrealistic and impossible sounding claims about a small stock, do not take their word for it. Do the research yourself and most of the time you will find yourself using the delete key.

I do not want to imply that all Internet-based research on low-priced stocks or advisory services devoted to low-priced stocks are bad. I run such a service myself and I know several other reputable conscientious folks who do the same. The best defense against being taken advantage of in the stock market is to do the homework yourself and check the facts before you buy the story! You will quickly be able to see who is trying to make you money and who is trying to rip you off.

Homework Pays

One other risk in the search for low-priced winning stocks is the fact that many low-priced stocks deserve to be low priced. These issues can frequently be on their way to zero. You always want to do the research as I have outlined. Can the company pay the bills or is bankruptcy a real possibility? Is this a distressed stock that has a solid turnaround plan or a company that is going to wipe out equity investors? All companies that go bankrupt see their stock trade down into the single digits on the way to zero.

If you see allegations of accounting or securities fraud in a company's reports, it is best just to take a pass on that issue even if you think there is potential. Unless you are a very experienced forensic accountant or securities attorney, it becomes very difficult to decipher exactly how these cases will end. Lots of people thought companies like Enron and WorldCom would be able to survive after the initial fraud allegations were revealed. They were not and a lot of people lost a lot of money.

Another minefield is trading in shares of companies that have filed bankruptcy. Odds are that all the assets of the company are going to bond holders and stockholders will be wiped out. I am always amazed by companies in bankruptcy that trade millions of shares in the days before the shares are delisted! The vast majority of the time equity is wiped out in a bankruptcy. On the rare occasions where it is not, a little research will show the potential winners. Insiders and large hedge funds will be buying the equity in big chunks to cash in on the bankruptcy reorganization. In the absence of this type of buying by insiders and big investors, avoid stocks in companies going through a bankruptcy reorganization or liquidation.

Cost Control

A factor you have to watch carefully when investing and trading low-priced stocks is costs and commissions. Many firms charge much higher commission rates for lower-priced issues so you need to be aware what your broker is charging you to invest. If you use margin borrowing in your trading activities be aware that some lower-priced stocks are not eligible for margin borrowing or are subject to higher interest rates. I hope you make searching for low-priced breakout stocks one of your core investment practices but make sure your brokerage firm is not penalizing you for searching for the outsized profit potential these stocks offer.

Also be aware that using a market order to buy and sell some low-priced shares can cost you money. The reason has to do with high spreads in some low-priced issues. The spread is the difference between the bid, or price someone is willing to buy shares from you, and the ask, the price where someone is willing to sell you shares. In a large liquid stock like IBM (IBM) this spread is usually around a penny. The cost is minimal. However on less heavily traded, lower-priced stock these spreads can be much wider. If you find an undiscovered growth stock, for example, that is not widely followed always check the bid and ask prices and consider using a limit order to trade the shares. Be aware of how many shares usually trade a day and try not to enter orders large enough to disrupt the trading of the stock. If you have to, break your orders into pieces and fill them a little at a time. Usually this will not be an issue but you have to be aware of those instances where it is or you can end up losing money.

Common Sense Prevents Pain

The key to avoiding risks in the stock market, especially low-priced stock, is to use common sense. No one is going to send you an email to tell you all about a stock that is going to make you rich beyond your wildest dreams. As I have said earlier in this book, finding these gems takes work and effort on your part and no one is going to give you the keys to the kingdom with no effort or cost on your part. Keep in mind, if your Uncle Fred were really a great stock picker he would not borrow $100 every time you see him. Read the 10Q and 10K, go through the financials, and read management's discussion of the business. Check the footnotes for warning signs and red flags.

Most of the time the alleged risks of low-priced stocks are just that—alleged. If you find a stock with the right financial and business characteristics the risks are actually nonexistent. It is the perception of greatly increased risks with low-priced stocks that is creating the opportunities for us to earn breakout profits.

Breakout Summary: Read the Warning Signs

- The best way to avoid getting caught up in this type of fraud is to avoid the come-ons and advertisements for companies you have never heard of, or are recommended by someone you have also never heard of.

- Many firms charge much higher commission rates for lower-priced issues so you need to be aware what your broker is charging you to invest. Be aware if you use margin borrowing in your trading activities that some lower-priced stocks are not eligible for margin borrowing or are subject to higher interest rates.

- Another potential cost you have to be aware of is the potential costs incurred by high spreads in some low-priced issues. The spread is the difference between the bid, or price someone is willing to buy shares from you, and the ask, the price where someone is willing to sell you shares.

Chapter Twelve

Low Prices and High Profits

Putting It All Together

HOPEFULLY I HAVE GIVEN YOU THE TOOLS AND information you need to begin investing in the exciting world of low-priced breakout stocks. Over my years in and around the financial markets I have found this to be the single best area for investors to earn explosive gains in stocks. It is even more true today, as trading of higher-priced larger companies is dominated by short-term traders and computerized traders. It is almost impossible for you and I to gain an advantage trading shares of behemoths like Wal-Mart (WMT) and IBM (IBM). These companies have dozens of analysts following their every move and thousands of traders are in and out of these stocks every day. It becomes very difficult for us to make money in these stocks and the high stock price means tying up large amounts of money to buy a meaningful stake in the company.

Simple laws of supply and demand help make lower-priced stocks more explosive in nature. It just takes less money to move a $6 stock in a $250 million company than it does a $60 stock in a $25 billion company. By focusing our research efforts on lower-priced companies we can gain an advantage that helps earn superior returns and reach our financial goals and dreams sooner than owning larger stocks or index funds. By getting ahead of Wall Street in lower-priced stocks we benefit from the institutional pack mentality that dominates many traditional investment managers. When they are selling and pushing stocks to low prices, we are buying. Then, when their excitement for these stocks return, we are selling to them. We are finding solid growth stocks before Wall Street notices and will see our stocks soar when they show up on the Street's radar screen. There simply is no better way for individual investors to outperform the market in my opinion.

Optimistic Profits

One of the most important takeaways I hope you have from this little book is that an optimistic approach to the markets will serve you a lot better as an investor than being overly fearful. Fear sells and often the media will hype all the problems with the world, the markets, and individual companies. If you focus on the fear you miss opportunities. If you focused on all that was wrong with the auto industry in 2008, you would have totally missed the fact that Ford was in fine shape and stood to benefit from the problems of its competitors. If you gave up when Dendreon got the first delay from the FDA, you would have missed some spectacular gains by never investigating further to discover that it was just a delay and approval for their cancer drug was probably forthcoming.

The same applies to the stock market itself. Markets are going to have declines. There will be recessions and bear markets throughout your career. The right way to look at these occasions is as inventory creation events, not catastrophes. One of the biggest advantages to buying lower-priced stocks is that as the stock market climbs there are fewer opportunities or solid companies trading in single digits. As a result, the approach tends to perform a measure of market timing for your portfolio. As prices climb you are usually selling earlier discoveries at a profit and are not able to find enough ideas to get fully reinvested much of the time. As a result you will usually have cash available to go bargain hunting when the market inevitably reverses course and declines.

There is another advantage to owning low-priced stocks when the market corrects. Many of these stocks are fallen angels or growth companies that stumbled briefly, driving the stock below $10. Wall Street and the big institutions already sold their shares and your stocks will not experience the type of selling pressure higher-priced issues are experiencing. When the large leveraged investors, like hedge funds, need to sell stocks they sell the higher priced more liquid issues to meet margin calls, not lower-priced smaller companies. So not only does the selling not hit your stocks as hard as the big names, they often push the big companies down to where they become inventory for you!

The best investors fit into the category that I like to call optimistic cynics. They are well aware that every bear market has ended and every economic recession has been followed by an economic recovery. They also know that the world is full of entrepreneurs and innovators who will discover new solutions to old problems and the world gets better over time throughout history. They know that companies that are out of favor today are often tomorrow's darlings. In the stock market, optimism pays off over time. It always has and always will.

The cynical part comes from not taking anyone's word for anything. Trust but verify is the order of the day. Great investors do not act on tips, rumors, or sales pitches. By doing their research and homework they avoid many of the mistakes investors can make that will damage their net worth. They dig into the financial filings and company presentations to determine what is really going on with the company and the likelihood they can recover or continue to grow. When markets are soaring and everyone is piling into stocks, great investors ask the most critical question of all: *Is it really different this time?* When markets are collapsing they ask themselves if the world is really ending. The answers to those questions help to temper your enthusiasm at market tops and turn your fear into action at market bottoms.

Read for Fun and Profit

Successful investors read voraciously to keep up with the world and the markets. Charlie Munger, the legendary investor who has been Warren Buffett's partner for decades, once said that he knew no wise people who did not read. Today with the Internet it is easier than ever to read a wide range of business and economic news with relative ease and timeliness. I always tell people to not just read those who agree with your view of the world, the markets, and stocks, but to also read everyone who disagrees with you as well. Reviewing an opposing view can point out any holes in your thought process and can often confirm and strengthen your opinion as well when you find flaws in their thought process. *Read everything you can as often as you can is some of the best advice I can give you about successful investing.*

Investing in low-priced breakout stocks can be one of the most profitable things you ever do, but throughout the book I have strived to avoid creating the impression that it is the easiest thing you will ever do. There is work involved. It is not back breaking and, unless you do your homework in the sauna, you should not have to break a sweat in your efforts. When you uncover a company that looks like a low-priced winner you have to go read the 10Q and 10K reports. Pay special attention to the footnotes and they will often help you discover potential problems or time bombs in the books. Always go to the company website to see if there is a presentation in the investor's relations section. These presentations can give you excellent insights into management's plans, as well as potential new products, services, or markets that may cause revenues and profits to explode. I probably read through four or five company's filings and presentations for every one that I buy. You will no doubt find the same: Doing the homework and in-depth research allows you to focus on buying the best stocks you can find.

Spend a few minutes to discover who is buying or selling the stock. If insiders are buying in the open market this indicates a high degree of management confidence in the future and verifies your strong opinion of the stock. If clusters of insiders are selling, especially at a low price, you may well have missed something and want to recheck your conclusions. If George Soros, David Tepper, and or other large successful investors are buying a stock that you like, this can also serve as confirmation of your conclusions. If they or other successful fund managers have been dumping the stock, you want to ask yourself what they know that you do not.

Spread Out

One thing you want to keep in mind when building a portfolio of low-priced breakout stocks is to keep your portfolio diversified. While diversified can be an overused word, it can be important in a portfolio of these types of stocks. You do not want to own all biotech stocks or have a large percentage of your portfolio in any one industry. When that happens, you are subject to industry-specific risk and this could limit your gains and expose you to too much price volatility. When you find several candidates in one industry, pick the very best one or two stocks for your portfolio. This increases your chance of overall success. When I look at my portfolio right now I have biotech

[142] Big Profits from Small Stocks

companies, smartphone manufacturers, banks, hotel operators, scrap metal processors, and restaurants. Spread your investments across several different industries to maximize your opportunity for success.

When possible try to find companies that respond differently to economic and market events. Higher oil prices, for example, can be wonderful for oil companies. They are not as great for airlines that use a lot of fuel. If your list of potential stocks includes both, this can help introduce a level of diversification that helps ward off specific-event risk. If you own oil companies or too many airlines, a rise in the increase of oil could hurt your portfolio. Keeping a balance helps avoid this.

Building Portfolios to Build Your Dreams

Investing in low-priced potential breakout stocks is work. However it can increase your net worth quicker than almost any other effort applied to investing I am aware of. One investment like Priceline can make it easier to put the kids through college or retire a few years earlier. An investment in an undiscovered growth gem like Darling can pay for a dream vacation or even a dream home. If you are willing to work at it, investing in single-digit stocks should add many digits to your account values over time.

One of the things I have done is set up a companion website for this book. I have mentioned it throughout the book and provided the address for you: www.bigprofits fromsmallstocks.com. This site contains ideas and methods to help you find low-priced breakout stocks and I hope you use it often! As a thank you for reading this book, I've provided three of my current low-priced stock recommendations at the website. (Those of you with smart phones and tablets who have used the QR codes throughout have already gotten a sneak peek at the names of these stocks to buy. Or if you haven't used them yet, I've listed them again for you at the end of this chapter.) Consider these stocks the first building blocks in your low-priced stock portfolio.

But my sincere hope is that you won't stop there. Using the ideas and techniques outlined in this book can help you break away from the mediocre results that come from following traditional investment vehicles. It can also help you find exciting under-the-radar stocks when Wall Street either has not found them yet or just doesn't want them.

Investing in breakout low-priced stocks is simply one of the most profitable ways to invest that I have ever discovered. It is my fondest hope that this method rewards you as well as it has me over the years and that you are able to follow a low-priced path to enormous financial success.

Breakout Summary: Low Prices Bring Big Profits

- Remember to visit our website for more tips on investing in low priced breakout stocks: www.bigprofitsfromsmallstocks.com.

- As a thank you for reading this book, I've hand-picked three low-priced breakout stocks for you to buy now. You can access them via your smartphone or tablet device by scanning the codes below. (See the Appendix if this is your first time using these codes.) Or you can also go to our website.

- See you online!

1. Scan code to get my latest **Fallen Angel** recommendation.

2. Scan code to get my latest **Undiscovered Growth** recommendation.

3. Scan code to get my latest **Bargain Bin** recommendation.

Appendix
Getting Started with
Quick Response (QR)
Codes

———————— ❧ ————————

I AM THRILLED TO BE ABLE TO INCLUDE QUICK RESPONSE codes (more commonly called QR codes), in this little book. These next generation bar codes are a quick and simple way for you to access information—in this case my real-time stock recommendations—instantly, from your mobile device.

If you've never used QR codes before, this Appendix shows you how to use them in three simple steps:

1. Select a cell phone, tablet, or other mobile device with a camera.
2. Check your device to be sure you have a QR code scanner App. If you're not sure you have one, or you need to download one, go to the App Store for your particular device and search for QR code scanners. You'll find a number of free Apps you can readily download.
3. Place the camera of your mobile device over the QR code, so that it can scan the code. The downloaded App will read the code in a matter of seconds and display my named stock recommendation, instantly.

If you run into any technical issues, or you don't own a mobile device with a camera, don't worry! I've also posted the information from these QR codes at the website I've set up for readers of this little book: www.bigprofitsfromsmallstocks.com.

More from Hilary Kramer

~

HILARY KRAMER IS ALSO THE AUTHOR OF THREE INVESTING
newsletters:

HILARY KRAMER'S
GAME**CHANGERS** ▶
Profiting from Companies that Are Changing the Game

HILARY KRAMER'S
BREAKOUTSTOCKS UNDER $5
Finding Under the Radar Stocks Poised to Double

HILARY KRAMER'S
HIGH OCTANE STOCKS
The Best Trades and Options Plays for Quick Profits

To read sample issues of these newsletters, or to
learn more about Hilary Kramer, go to the website
www.gamechangerstocks.com.